# SOUTH PACIFIC

# SOUTH PACIFIC

## Jack and Dorothy Fields

THOSE WHO HELPED

TAHITI: "Teamo" Reitz, Aad van der Heyde, Kelley, Muk, and Jay, Harry and Helen Marsh

SAMOA: Ex-Governor H. Rex Lee, High Talking Chief Freddy and Pat Letuli, High Talking Chief Pele

TONGA: Ve'ehala, Keeper of the Palace Records, Oscar, and Emma

HAWAII: Richard MacMillian, Robert Goodman, Paul Kendell of Pan Am, and Roger Ritchie of Hawaiian Airlines

FIJI: Rob Wright

NEW HEBRIDES: Reece Discombe, Bob Paul

NEW CALEDONIA: Bruno Tabuteau, Mr. Martinet

NEW GUINEA: Bill Stokes

MICRONESIA: Jim Boykin, Bob Owens, Peter Wilson, Jim Murray, Russ & Verna Curtis, Robert Shoecraft, Ex-High Commissioner Bill Norwood, Chiefs of Bikini, King of Ulithi

Hal Roth for the loan of his "stone-fishing" pictures
Charles Regal and Hal Wagner of Matson Lines
David Nelson of the old South Pacific Airlines
Frank Ladik and Bruce Plowman of Continental Airlines
Air crews and ground personnel of Air Micronesia
Bali Hai Hotel, Moorea
Pago Pago Intercontinental Hotel, Samoa

The National Geographic Society for allowing use of my picture of the ribbon-tailed bird of paradise

A special thanks to all those islanders who gave us moments from their lives that we might photograph them.

Previous page: Cook's Bay, Moorea, Society Islands.

Distributors

Continental Europe
BOXERBOOKS, INC.
Zurich

Canada
FITZHENRY & WHITESIDE LIMITED
Ontario

The Far East
JAPAN PUBLICATIONS TRADING CO.
P.O. Box 5030 Tokyo International, Tokyo

# Contents

# Oceania

The first white man to view the Pacific Ocean was Vasco Nuñez de Balboa. After slashing his way westward through the jungle barriers of the Isthmus of Panama, in September, 1513, he suddenly sighted the great body of water. Falling to his knees, he claimed all the lands it touched in the name of his monarch, Ferdinand the Catholic of Spain. He called it the "Great South Sea." He never knew that it covers a third of the planet's surface—seventy million square miles—or that from where he stood China lay eleven thousand miles due west. He never knew that he was many millennia late in discovering it.

Seven years later, Fernando Magellan tried to find a route to the East Indies through the obstacle of the Americas. He left his name to the watery hell off South America's tip—the Straits of Magellan—and, sailing into the sudden tranquillity of Balboa's Great South Sea, renamed it "Pacific Ocean"—calm, peaceful. He believed it empty of land, as well he might; he sailed across it for three months without landing on a single one of the Pacific's thousands of islands, until he came to Guam and the Marianas.

But the Melanesian people were the first-comers to the Oceanic empire; then came Micronesians, then Polynesians. Sailing intrepidly across the Pacific, these peoples, named for the three great areas of Oceania, discovered the wide-flung tropic islands and made them their own.

Not all the islands of Oceania fit the paradise image of waving palms, sweeping beaches, and crystalline lagoon waters, nor fulfill the fables of lands where sweet fruits await plucking and all pleasures of life come easily. Yet the dreams of city dwellers and those deep within the borders of continents are filled with a siren call to these bits of land that dot the Pacific. Today, many thousands of people are done with wishing and are whisking off in jet planes to experience their dream islands—whether tropic paradise, wild jungle, or flat, coral atoll—to sample the way of life of peoples who live intimately with the wind, the sun, and the sea.

Opposite: From a jet aircraft somewhere over Polynesia.

This book is dedicated to the island people of the Pacific—with love, appreciation, and great respect.

# Melanesia

# Melanesia

GILBERT ISLANDS

EQUATOR

ADMIRALTY ISLANDS

NEW IRELAND

NEW GUINEA

WEST IRIAN

NORTHEAST NEW GUINEA

NEW BRITAIN

Mt. Hagen

PAPUA

SOLOMON ISLANDS

Port Moresby

ELLICE ISLANDS

SANTA CRUZ ISLANDS

WALLIS ISLAND

Darwin

Espiritu Santo Island

NEW HEBRIDES

Malekula

Efate

FIJI

Vanua Levu

Taveuni

Yasawa Group

Viti Levu

Lau Group

Ouvéa Atoll

Erromango

Sava

Mouly Atoll

Tanna

Ovalau

AUSTRALIA

NEW CALEDONIA

Aneityum

Nouméa

TROPIC OF CAPRICORN

Isle of Pines

South  Pacific  Ocean

KERMADEC ISLANDS

Sydney

TASMANIA

Wellington

NEW ZEALAND

# Melanesia

These strange, haunting dark islands rising in silhouettes against the Pacific's wide sky sprawl between the equator to the north and the Tropic of Capricorn to the south and include a wealth of differing lands, but almost all are crested with rugged mountains. New Guinea has snow-capped interior peaks falling away to steamy mangrove swamps along its river-riddled shores; the Solomon Islands, with their hot, humid, malarial jungles, are remembered in nightmares by many veterans of the battle for Guadalcanal; the New Hebrides, some of whose islands are punctuated with fiery volcanos while others lie smothered under hilly carpets of dense forests; New Caledonia, a long loaf-shaped island cleft by mountain ridges, half the land a dry and arid beige, the other half wet and lush green; and Fiji, a sprinkling of verdant bits of earth that look as though they had been spun off two larger center islands. These are the islands that Europeans named Melanesia—"Black Islands"—from the Greek, *melas*, "black," and *nesos*, "island." These are the lands that claim the majority of Oceania's people.

Melanesians—the dark people. Sometimes called Oceanic Negroids, they are as varied physically, culturally, and spiritually as their islands. These were the forbidding Stone Age savages and cannibals that scared away foreign explorers and settlers long after other Pacific islanders acknowledged their new "masters." No one knows for sure how many ethnic groups there are in Melanesia. In New Guinea alone over seven hundred different languages are spoken as well as uncounted dialects. Even today tribes are still being "discovered." Not long ago, in the highlands of New Guinea, the Australian administration agreed to acquit several tribesmen charged with killing and eating an enemy. They were acquitted on the grounds that "such is the custom among them."

To the first foreign invaders all Melanesians presented one dominant trait—aggressive hostility. Brotherhood among men was not the Melanesian life-style. For millennium after millennium, clans (related families) and tribes (people related by language and custom) had held themselves apart. Every stranger was suspect, often automatically an enemy. Elaborate preparations for war and fighting punctuated the old way of life.

And life followed patterns—a ritualistic pattern from their past for each tribe, guided by ghosts of their ancestors, who from supernatural fastnesses kept watch on the living, disciplining them and guiding their destinies. Even the newly deceased were not considered really dead, but recognized in a different role as new members of an ever increasing spirit world. Melanesians generally believed that although human bodies die and decay, the spirits are eternal and their continuity can be assured through the birth of children. There are many spirits, for there have been many ancestors, and these countless, immemorial dead (speaking through mediums) direct the activities of the tribe; they are alert to any infraction of clan or tribal law or tradition, rite or ritual and are ready to punish it with a crop failure or a defeat in war or some other disaster until—through corrective ritual—things are set right again. Each clan, each tribe departs from custom at its peril; the only safe ways are the old and known ways. This is still for some, and was once for all, the basic unity of life and worship in Melanesia.

And many still practice, as formerly nearly all did, initiation and fertility rites and rituals to ensure abundance of everything by which wealth and power were measured—from harvests of yams and taro to success in hunting and fishing, from pig reproduction to human birth. All rituals are funded or sacrifices are made in whatever currency or method of sacrifice is the tribal custom. For some it might be exchanging precious and rare seashells, or gigantic yams, or it might be the trading or sacrificing of pigs, or an elaborate feast, a sing-sing. For others certain rituals demanded a human sacrifice, perhaps a captive enemy, perhaps a passing stranger, perhaps a member of the tribe itself whom the spirits designated for reasons of their own. Black magic—sorcery —once widely practiced, has been outlawed throughout Melanesia by the foreign occupying powers, but it still continues on most of the islands in an underground fashion. Cause of death by a verbal or symbolic "weapon" is difficult to prove in a modern court of law.

The constant wars between tribal villages called for the aid of spirit ancestors, but battles were never fought to gain new converts to a differing belief, nor to gain an extensive "kingdom"; war was simply the way of life. Sometimes after hours of posturing, the "war" ended as soon as the first wound was inflicted or the first death sustained. Avenging of the casuality was sure to be followed, perhaps not until years later, by a "payback" war or death. Tribal or clan leadership was not hereditary: each leader earned the favor of his fellows by personal merit or his ability to acquire wealth.

Captured enemies were treated differently by different tribes; some victims were eaten, sometimes by the entire clan or tribe, sometimes only by the conquering warriors, or the warriors might eat just one special organ—the heart, say, in the belief that it would increase their own bravery. A few clans ate their own people after death, acting on much the same belief—that the strength, wisdom, and spirit of the deceased would become literally a part of the whole clan and so would not be lost. An almost diametrically opposite belief was held by other tribes, for whom the eating of an enemy was an act of hatred, an expression of utter contempt. Still other Melanesian groups hunted and ate human beings more casually than they did other game, for wild animals are almost totally absent from the islands of Oceania. Many tribes who considered eating human flesh revolting nonetheless made fetishes of skulls or bones or sometimes entire bodies of tribal members or tribal enemies, ritually preparing and preserving them. All these forms of ancestor worship kept the islanders confined on their ancestral lands. The longer a tribe lived in a particular place, the stronger grew the power of its spirit-world, the more irresistible the tie to the land itself, the more the taboos affecting their daily life.

These superstitious islanders so closely shackled to the fierce spirit-world of their ancestors did not take kindly to the arrival of white men. Few Melanesians reacted with anything but hostility, since it seemed obvious that these pale-skinned invaders with odd-shaped heads and removable skins (for so hats and clothing were first interpreted) could only be evil spirits returned to life. Most likely they were ancestors come to vent malice or administer punishment, the kind of unfriendly spirits who had in the past haunted the tribespeople.

White men could only be dangerous. The Melanesians, therefore, to protect their ancestral lands, embarked upon a sacred battle. They took up their bows and arrows, or their spears, or clubs, or slingshots, and tried to drive the "evil spirits" away. Their attacks brought terrible repercussions—warriors fell dead as the intruders pointed a "magic stick" and caused it to blaze fire and smoke and roar like thunder. Surely such beings were supernatural evil spirits with supreme potency!

Gradually, however, it became evident that these were not spirits at all, for, if they were taken by surprise and clubbed from behind, their heads cracked open and they died. These strange beings must be men also, but men who possessed miraculous magic sticks, strong steel axes, lengths of bright red cloth, beautiful beads and shells. Some tribes coveted these desirable possessions to the point of frenzy, and to gain them they would do anything—pretend friendship, then murder and rob; barter; sell clan members into slavery; supply women for the foreigners' strange sexual habits; and sometimes even exchange a precious bit of ancestral land. The Melanesians' reputation for savage treachery spread throughout the Western world, and only the most daring adventurers and outlaws braved the bloodthirsty peoples of the "Black Islands."

Then came new kinds of white men to Melanesia. They had no guns; they brought nothing much to trade. After they learned the villagers' language they told them that just about everything the islanders were doing—eating enemies, placating spirits, having more than one wife, wearing leaves instead of cloth, dancing, drinking palm toddy—was altogether sinful. Unless they changed their ways, they were warned, fearful disasters would strike them down and the tribe would be doomed forever to a horrible place these gunless strangers called Hell.

The Melanesians were quick to discover that, being gunless, missionaries were easy to kill. But as each one was dispatched, another arrived to take his place, and when he had been taken care of, there came still another, equally determined to change the old tribal laws. And finally even these men, too, came with guns to Melanesia. . . .

# New Guinea

On a map it resembles a foraging dinosaur, a *Tyrannosaurus rex* perhaps, with its dome-shaped head facing west, just missing the equator, its great maw open to gobble up bits of the Indonesian Archipelago, its distended body bellying toward the northern finger of Australia, its tail lashing the Coral Sea. This is the outline of New Guinea—second largest island in the world.

A hundred million years or so ago, this great land was part of a continent that swept out from Asia, up from Australia to the North Pacific's Marianas, and far enough east and south to include Fiji, New Caledonia, and New Zealand. Then the ocean floor shifted and heaved up mountains; temperatures changed drastically; ice caps melted, then froze, and melted again; sea levels rose and fell. These convulsions gave birth to New Guinea—and now it is home to nearly two-thirds of the total population of Oceania, some three million people in all; and they, too, have an ancient ancestry.

In the time before man measured time nomadic hunters and food-gatherers came to New Guinea. These first inhabitants were short, dark-skinned, woolly-haired Negritos and Australoids for whom the process of migration occupied countless generations. Around twenty-five thousand years ago, during the last glacial period, they fled from the growing cold in the rain forests of Asia (and, some say, Africa) and funneled into the tropic warmth of the Malay Peninsula. As short, harsh generations passed, the nomad families, using rafts and simple bark canoes, crossed channels (narrower then than now) between Indonesian islands and landed finally on New Guinea. These pioneers domesticated no animals, they grew no crops, they used only chipped stone tools. Some found the shallow land bridge to Australia and moved over it to inhabit the earth's smallest continent. By the beginning of the fifth millennium B.C. rising seas had severed the land link between island and continent. The descendants of these earliest Stone Age castaways remain today as the Australian Aborigines.

Around the same time, new immigrants began coming to New Guinea, bringing with them knowledge that the resident nomadic Negritos had never acquired—agriculture and the ability to make polished stone tools and weapons. Continuing waves of newcomers found the island a good place to plant the tubers and feed the pigs they had brought with them. Some settled along the swampy shores, others climbed beyond the high, cloud-capped mountains and in the course of time forgot the sea even existed. Still others paddled narrow dugouts far up steaming coastal rivers. They were dark-skinned too, these new arrivals, but they were taller than the first inhabitants and they were stronger and more aggressive. The nomadic clans retreated into remote mountains, taking with them newly gained knowledge of food growing and the skill of making polished stone tools.

Later, other migrants—brown-skinned Malay-Mongoloid Micronesians and paler-skinned Caucasian-featured Polynesians—stayed along New Guinea shores, but then sailed north or east toward destinations known alone to them and their guiding gods.

The first Westerner to sight New Guinea was a Portuguese navigator who sailed past the island's northern coast in 1512 but noted it only casually, for his destination was the magnificent riches of the East Indies. Fourteen years later another Portuguese reached New Guinea—he took time to observe the inhabitants and to christen the island *Ilhas dos Papuas* ("Island of the Frizzle-Haired"). Today the remnant "Papua" remains as the name of one of its territories. Another title was bestowed the following year by the Spanish traveler Alvaro de Saavedra, who called it *Isla del Oro* ("Island of Gold"); but that name was replaced in 1545 when still another Spanish navigator likened the islanders to the people of the Guinea coast of Africa, called it New Guinea, and claimed it for Spain.

The name stuck but the claim did not. The Dutch, the British, and the Germans all ignored the claim during succeeding centuries: each sent expeditions to explore the island from time to time and sometimes halfheartedly announced annexations. In 1793 the British East India Company took possession of a section of New Guinea, but the homeland failed to recognize the company's claim; ninety years later, a British magistrate hoisted the Union Jack at Port Moresby, but again London declined to take any official interest.

Europeans were not much taken with settling New Guinea. The humid lowlands fostered malaria and unknown fevers; its shores bristled with bowmen who considered all strangers fair game for the cooking pits. Crocodiles, virulently poisonous snakes, hordes of blood sucking leeches, clouds of mosquitoes lay in wait along the river channels, and everywhere jungle-snarled mountains rose to fortress an unknown interior.

The Dutch, however, in 1828, formally annexed the western half of the dinosaur-shaped island—its head and chest—then ignored it, favoring the more profitable Indonesian islands, which they had claimed in 1595. Then, in 1884, Germany took a sizeable bite from the northeastern section (which it called Kaiser Wilhelm Land), as well as laying claim to groups of adjoining islands—an act that prompted London, in November of that same year, to proclaim the southeastern part of the island as British New Guinea, a protectorate. Thus, as the nineteenth century drew to a close, New Guinea was partitioned into three territories, the Dutch in the west, the Germans in the northeast, and the British in the southeast.

The latter territory was transferred in 1906 to the newly founded Commonwealth of Australia and renamed Papua; then, in 1914, when war broke out, Australian troops moved north and easily took over what had been German New Guinea. After the war, Australia administered the captured territory under a League of Nations mandate until 1942, when the Japanese captured most of the island. Today New Guinea is still partitioned into three, the two eastern sections being administered by Australia (the northeastern territory is a trusteeship of the United Nations), the west by Indonesia, which took it over from the Dutch in 1963. The border was then closed, making the new land of West Irian a forbidden territory.

Some confusion exists about the name New Guinea. The entire island is called thus, but the name also applies to the two territories under Australian control, Papua and the Trust Territory of New Guinea. (P-NG is becoming more popular as the designation today.) New Guinea is also the title of the northwestern territory, along with its more than six hundred offshore islands.

After World War I, a few hearty Australians learned to cope with the island's special frustrations and set up trading posts and copra plantations. Where saner men feared to tread, missionaries slogged into muggy hinterlands, eager for martyrdom and Christian converts, and often finding the former but seldom the latter. Competition for heathen souls became so fierce that the Australian government had to intervene, assigning different areas to the London Missionary Society, the Anglicans, the Wesleyans, and the Roman Catholics.

But still the towering mountains guarded the secret heart of the island. Knife-edged, perpetually cloud-hung, they were impenetrable to the white man, presumably uninhabited, and—most damaging epithet of all in the European vocabulary—unprofitable. Then, in 1921, a single word, whispered at first, then shouted around the world became the key unlocking the mountain fortresses.

GOLD!

In February, 1926, a pair of Australians, Royal and Glasson, stumbled up a tributary of the Bulolo River to a place called Edie Creek. There, at an altitude of sixty-five hundred feet, they struck it rich. Saavedra's *Isla del Oro* had earned the prophetic name he gave it in 1528.

The rush was on. Driven men chasing rainbows mired through hot, malarial swamps, up rain-slimy trails, where they shivered in the high air's biting cold and waited tensely for a sudden ambush by silent bowmen with poison-tipped arrows. Edie Creek became big business. Airports were built at Lae on the coast and Wau inland, so planes could airlift heavy dredging equipment to the gold sites, which soon became the world's largest air-freight operation. This was the new frontier, and the airplane cut supply-line time from over a week's grueling uphill toil to a twenty-minute flight.

Among the many who were lured by the glint of gold was a young railway clerk from Queensland, Michael Leahy, who was twice granted claims on Edie Creek and who twice lost them because of illness. But his greatest fever knew no cure—gold fever. So when, in 1930, he heard of a new strike on the Ramu River, he wondered if there might be a richer source in the river's headwaters hidden somewhere behind Mt. Wilhelm, the territory's tallest peak, over fifteen thousand feet.

To find his beckoning pot of gold, Leahy proposed to do what no one had dared before—to explore "one of the world's last great mysteries," as he was later to describe it in a book he coauthored with Maurice Crain, *The Land That Time Forgot*. Accompanied by sixteen porters, he and Mick Dwyer, another gold seeker, inched up a jungle-coated flank of the Bismarck range toward a geographical question mark. Behind the sawtoothed ridges they shared moments of mutual surprise with unnamed tribes.

Trading "miraculous" steel tools and colorful beads for food, escorted and passed along from village to village in hopeful pursuit of nugget-laden rivers, Leahy and Dwyer received another surprise—there were no rivers of gold. They pushed on, totally lost, but seven hard weeks later they found themselves near a sawmill on the Purari River, near the Gulf of Papua. The final surprise came when they realized they had walked across New Guinea, from north to south, straight through that blank map space marked UNEXPLORED.

For the next four years, Leahy, accompanied by his three brothers, investigated the unknown highlands. They were still looking for gold, but at the same time they were laying bare the secret heart of New Guinea, where half a million undiscovered aboriginal inhabitants still dwelt in isolation. The expeditions, in Leahy's words, "laid to rest for all time the theory that the center of New Guinea is a mass of uninhabitable mountains."

In December, 1934, they led the expedition to investigate the reported murders of two prospector friends, Jack and Tom Fox, and, at the same time, complete their aborted gold search. An hour out of camp, a runner told them that the supposedly murdered men were alive at a nearby bush church. When the Leahys reached it, the Fox brothers, bony thin, weak from hunger and exhaustion still managed to whisper the news—"not enough gold in the lot of it to fill a tooth." The rainbow chasing had ended.

Just thirty-three years later, we flew over the green razorback ridges that had challenged the Leahys and other men of adventure. Carefully the pilot slid the plane through a slot in the mountain slopes, and then we zoomed low over the Waghi Valley toward Mt. Hagen.

The town is named for the territory's second tallest peak, 13,120-foot Mt. Hagen. When the Leahys first came here, a generation ago, the outside world was totally unaware of the existence of this rich, heavily populated valley. Now the town of Mt. Hagen boasts a hotel, a couple of motels, a country club, and a nine-hole golf course, and, nearby, the ever-important airport. The electricity functions most of the time, the telephone some of the time. The town's six hundred European residents have been carefully screened by the authorities before being issued permits to settle.

We discovered that Danny Leahy (who was barely out of his teens when he had walked into this valley) was still there, living on a farm five miles away. He is white haired now, and his sight is bad, for he was nearly blinded and partially deafened during the extreme hardships of the war. As we sat in the screened-in living room, drinking tea and listening to the drone of the cicadas, he reminisced about one of his wartime tasks. He was sent to rescue five nuns, a Jesuit brother, and a priest who were trapped by advancing Japanese troups in the Sepik River Mission on the coast. They had only one way to escape—through a swampland maze then up over the jungle-choked mountains to the patrol outpost airstrip at Mt. Hagen. It took them three months.

The days of gold and glory are gone. Danny Leahy grows livestock—pigs, cattle, sheep—crops of soybeans, corn, peanuts, but mostly coffee and some tea.

"Yes, there's still some gold out there," Danny claimed, sweeping his hand toward the valley, "but with my eyes... I can't see well enough now...."

Jack Fox, too, came back to the valley after the war. When we were there, he was working at the government agricultural station, which is experimenting with new plants and carefully introducing them into the highlands. One is pyrethrum, an ingredient of insecticides; another is passion fruit, which is grown by local tribes, then processed, and the juice shipped to Australia; tea is perhaps most promising of all the new crops.

Another pioneer who stayed is Father Ross, a nonstop, mighty-mite man barely five feet tall, but quick on the draw with Bible and cross. He and two others practically heel-stepped the Leahy expedition into the Waghi Valley. The murder in 1935 of his two compatriots, added to previous killings by the aggressive highlanders, led authorities to close the area to unauthorized explorations and settling. Since World War II, foreigners have been allowed to make temporary visits.

The Catholic mission near the former airstrip (now golf course) is Father Ross's kismet.

"Oh, I left once," he told us, "went back to the States on leave—saw lots of ball games—had to shave off my beard—it was dark brown then and down to here—" chopping his hand edgewise at his waist. "When I got back nobody knew me—it grew back all right—but completely white! Can't afford to leave again—who knows what'd happen next time!"

Some thirty miles north of Mt. Hagen in a bower of green jungle is the Baiyer River Birds of Paradise Sanctuary. For centuries the birds have been hunted for their plumes, so that now some species are near extinction. Malay hunters would venture deep into western New Guinea's mountains to start the plumes on Asian trade routes, where the feathers sometimes ended up in the turbans of sultans or maharajahs, or rivaled the jewels in the royal crown of Nepal. From the East Indies, the Spanish and Portuguese sent the beautifully plumed skins (with wings and feet removed) as kingly gifts to the Iberian monarchs. And what a royal puzzlement they were! The Portuguese decided that these "wingless" birds glided always upward toward the sun, propelled by their long tails, never touching earth until they fell dead. The Spanish disagreed—they claimed these were birds of an earthly paradise that flew only when the winds blew—and thus they were named: birds of paradise.

As late as 1913, Germany had a thriving industry exporting plumes for the European millinery market. Today there is a strict law against the selling of plumes by either Europeans or Asians—a five hundred dollar fine per feather and confiscation.

Nature's whole reason for all the fine feathers is the wooing and winning of the usually drab, shy female. Prancing, dancing, flashing rainbow plumes in the sun, the male displays in his territorial arena. Once the affair is consummated, he flits away to woo another. The hen lays her single egg and sets—perchance to dream of her dazzling, fickle lover.

Hundreds, nay—thousands—of brilliant plumes flash in the intense mountain sunlight, bouncing and waving in hypnotic kaleidoscopes of color—it is the annual Highland sing-sing. Held alternately at Mt. Hagen and Goroka (forty-five miles east), the festival lasts for two days and attracts some sixty thousand participants from over four hundred tribes—the largest intertribal gathering in the world.

The people come from over the mountain walls, from the remotest valleys, sometimes walking for weeks in order to take part in the dancing, singing, drumming, and chanting, or merely to watch and be watched—for that is the way of a sing-sing, a ritual by the living to remember the past and to ensure the future.

They come for the thrill of dancing out a make-believe victory, now that the old wars are done and intertribal feuding is settled by patrol officers or courts of law instead of "payback" battles. Some are first-generation noncannibals; but the elders remember when neighbor hunted neighbor, and they dance like raiding warriors. Those who scorned cannibalism dance a fertility rite, asking the spirits for a wealth of pigs and for prosperous gardens. Some dance out the posturings of birds and animals, and some do not dance at all, but stand shy and quiet, close to government patrol officers who have brought them here for their first startled look at a strange new world. Lifted by planes and helicopters into the unknown space beyond their cloistered mountain worlds, they are Stone Age astronauts taking one small step forward for themselves, one giant leap forward for their clans.

# New Hebrides

"What do you opt for," asked the immigration official at the airport, "British or French?"

"Oh, either one," I replied airily, unsure exactly what he meant and having no desire to precipitate an international incident.

"Do you," he went on, "speak French?"

I told him that I did not.

"Then you'd better opt British," he said, banging a stamp down onto a page of my passport. "Now you're subject to British law, you can use Australian money, and if you get sick, check in at the British hospital. Have a nice time."

This was my introduction to the unique condominium government of the New Hebrides, whose eighty-odd islands are administered jointly by Great Britain and France from Port Vila on the island of Efate.

The islands are volcanic, lying in a slanting Y-shaped chain, 450 miles long, at the juncture of the Coral Sea and the open ocean. Volcanic violence keeps creating new islets. Even during one of our short visits, a lava island the size of a football field emerged from boiling seas, stinking of sulphur, and staining the waves with the excrement of island birth. Efate is at the junction of the Y, about fifteen hundred miles northeast of Sydney and 750 miles due west of Fiji. Vila, as it is more often called, is a town of about thirty-five hundred people with a sleepy, tropic isle charm about it. The main street curves along the bay, its shops facing the sunset, while immediately behind them rise steep green hills studded with white houses. Capping a hilltop are the French government offices, whose flag flies precisely at the same height as that of the British government on its grounds nearby. The creaking bureaucracy struggling under three sets of laws issuing from French, British, and condominium governments exists to prevent some four thousand French and about two thousand British citizens from mutual exploitation. The Joint Administration, or condominium, concerns itself with local situations that lie outside the jurisdiction of the two National Services. It submits its yearly budget in British currency, while Australian dollars and French Oceanic francs are the islands' "everyday" money. Laws are enforced by dual New Hebridean police forces, each in the uniform of one of the two joint powers, and each maintains its own courts and prisons. Foreigners, called *ressortissants*, a term that includes temporary visitors and tourists, must chose to come under the wing of either British or French law. These *ressortissants* also include several hundred Wallis Islanders, Tahitians, Vietnamese, and other French colonists, while the British count Gilbertese, Tongans, Fijians, Chinese, and Fijian Indians on their lists. As for seventy thousand New Hebrideans, who share their islands with the "aliens," they owe allegience to neither power—they have no recognized national identity.

New Hebrideans are diverse types of Melanesians, including some pygmy tribes who live in remote mountains on Santo (the largest island and the location of the islands' only other town, Luganville). A couple of the islands have Polynesian clans, left over from some past migration. Carbon-dating testifies that the islands were inhabited by the beginning of the first millennium B.C., but how the people got there from their ancestral land, New Guinea, is a question open to speculation.

Nevertheless, there they were in the year 1606, when the Spaniard Quiros came by in his Pacific Ocean quest for the "lost" continent of Terra Australis. Sure that he had reached his goal at what is now the island of Santo, he named it *Terra Australis del Espiritu Santo*, taking possession of it as well as all land lying from where he stood to the South Pole in the name of Spain and the Catholic Church. On this proclamation site, he decreed, he would found the future capital, Nueva Jerusalem. To feast the declaration his crew journeyed inland to raid the villagers' gardens and pig herds. Originally the islanders had been friendly to these, the first white men they had ever seen, but after the raids, they sought reprisal—and were cut down by a fusillade of bullets. Like most Spanish explorers, Quiros had already left a trail of spilled blood as he had island-hopped his way across the Pacific. The New Hebrideans continued to resist until the Spanish sailed away, leaving the islanders to their desired isolation for the next 160 years.

Then, in the late eighteenth century, came a famous quartet of European navigators and explorers—Bougainville (who determined that the islands were not, after all, the continent of Australia); Captain Cook (who, with some fond memory of Scotland in mind, gave the islands their present name); Captain Bligh (who bobbed past after the mutiny on the *Bounty* but who wisely refrained from stopping); and the Comte de la Perouse (who disappeared there). None made friends with the islanders; instead they used their guns freely on the "bloodthirsty savages" and spread stories that kept other Europeans away for another generation.

But in 1825, on the island of Tanna, Captain Peter Dillon discovered virgin sandalwood forests, and for the next forty years, cutthroat sandalwood traders recklessly destroyed life and property in these lawless southern islands of the New Hebrides. After loading their holds with wood, some crews would casually murder and rape the very islanders who had helped them harvest the trees. They would burn the homes, ruin the gardens, destroy the pigs, cut down the coconut palms—all this to engender such intense hostility that no rival ships would dare put into that port; for the surviving villagers, weak in weapons but strong in their desire for revenge, would vent their fury on the next foreigners they encountered.

Into the midst of this murder and mayhem came the missionaries. Flushed with their easy successes in Polynesia they condemned themselves in the New Hebrides to a living hell that outdid the one they talked about from the pulpits. Fourteen years after sandalwood was discovered, Protestant Samoan converts were brought to Tanna as "teachers," while the Reverend John Williams of the London Missionary Society sailed on to Erromango, where he and his assistant were promptly killed on landing, as were their replacements. By 1871, six missionaries had gambled with their fate and lost.

Meanwhile, a Presbyterian minister had arrived on the southernmost island of Aneityum. He forced the islanders to wear European clothes, but to earn money for clothing, the people had to work for the hated sandalwooders, who then would turn traders and sell them shoddy goods. Thus the missionary, who blamed sandalwooders for both the ills and ill will of the islanders, himself aided his enemies. Clothing helped skin diseases, tuberculosis, and colds to spread, and influenza, measles, and whooping cough were quickly fatal to people with no immunity.

The island's population dropped steadily from twelve thousand to eight hundred by 1885. For his 350-member congregation, the reverend ordered a church built to seat one thousand.

The plagues of diseases caused some islanders to become devout worshipers seeking divine protection. Others, like the Erromangoans, who listened as the minister raved about sinning and how great pestilence would come from Heaven unless they repented, decided *he* personally, was responsible for the pestilence of measles that had killed one-third of the islanders, and murdered him and his wife. Measles had originally been carried to the neighboring island of Tanna by an ill Samoan aboard the London Missionary Society ship. The islands' population, which had once been estimated in millions, was down to approximately six hundred fifty thousand by 1871.

Eight years before, a new terror had begun for New Hebrideans—blackbirding. Thousands of young men were shanghaied or sold by their chiefs for guns, taken aboard "recruitment" ships, and carried off to strange lands to do the backbreaking labor that the growing of cotton and sugarcane once entailed. Most of them never saw their home islands again. Twenty years later Australia inaugurated its White Australia Policy to halt the cruel importing of Melanesian laborers; in Fiji, the settlers had found that Indians worked harder than Melanesians, and, by 1891, blackbirding had ended. The population of the New Hebrides was now below one hundred thousand.

With the depopulation of the islands, fertile but unused land invited foreign settlers, and vast copra plantations sprouted along the shores on land "purchased" from local chiefs. In view of the New Hebridean labor shortage, French plantation owners brought in workers from Vietnam, New Caledonia, and other French island colonies; the British did the same with Fijian, Tongan, and Gilbertese laborers. When, finally the Germans expressed an interest in the islands, John G. Paton, a Presbyterian missionary working on Tanna agitated for the British government to annex the islands before France could do so, for French plantation owners and missionaries also were interested in having France own these "unclaimed" islands. The result was the Joint Naval Commission set up by the two powers in 1886. Its shaky existence lasted until 1914, when it was replaced by an Anglo-French Protocol, which was finally accepted in 1923 and which has been in operation ever since. Neither government dares change the status quo for fear the whole structure will fall like a house of cards.

Today, for many New Hebrideans life remains a limbo. Education and health care in the rural areas are either nonexistent or in the hands of missionaries. Some tribes, like the Small Nambas and the Big Nambas of Malekula, retain their ways, rejecting intruders, although even they recently emerged from their retreats and made peace with their traditional enemies in order to honor Britain's Prince Philip with ceremonial dances.

In these islands, where soil is rich and food is easily grown and plentiful, the people developed cultures with complex systems of convention, ritual, and religion. While the cultures differ among the many clans and tribes in the New Hebrides, just as the languages do, the lives of the people on Malekula, Santo, Ambryum, and the smaller islands nearby for centuries have revolved (and still revolve) around the pig—not as a valuable food animal, but for the value attached to the size, shape, and condition of his tusks.

Pigs give life meaning and are the way to power—the goal of every man in a village. Beginning with ten borrowed pigs to use as a bride-price (for no man is suitable husband material without pigs), a man acquires not only a wife but a debt. His borrowed pigs keep increasing in value, simply because the tusks, regularly studied and measured (and for which there are fifty specially descriptive growth words), keep growing. The tusks, the lower canines, grow in circles, once the corresponding upper teeth are removed. After about seven years, a tusk will complete its first circle, and the boar will be fed special food, since the ivory, piercing the lower jaw, makes eating difficult. If the pig survives another seven years, his tusks will complete a second circle, making him virtually priceless. In rare instances, he might grow three circles, and then it will cost one pig admission just to look at this symbol of greatness, for such an animal is the power of the earth spirit itself.

The only way to get out of debt is to go into the pig business by lending out male piglets with their top teeth removed: the growing tusks increase the animals' value on someone else's food. By working on community projects for "pig" wages, and collecting "pig" dues when his sisters marry and when they beget sons, a man, after years of diligent effort, might be able to pay off his debt—provided all of his pigs have lived—for a dead pig is nothing; it is not even considered edible.

Since demand for pigs always exceeds supply, (female pigs are deemed worthless and are often slaughtered) and what with rites of passage—births, circumcisions, marriages, deaths—all requiring transactions in live pigs, once a man is out of debt, he can embark on his life's dream—full pig power. He will begin by lending out more valuable pigs, he will take more wives to tend his growing herd. Then, when the time is right, he will announce at a special yam feast the date when he will recall all of his pigs that are out on loan. This will be the first ritual step of his climb toward a topmost rank, where his spirit will become one with the totem hawk soaring high above the jungle. In some villages there are only five steps, in others as many as thirty-five, before the desired goal can be reached, but few men ever live to reach it.

The recall date is usually set two years ahead, so there will be time to grow a surplus of food to feed the hundreds who come for days of feasting and dancing. During the ceremonies, hundreds of tuskers will be aligned properly for the appropriate moment when the status-seeker will walk along the rows of tethered squealing boars, killing most of them with a single blow between the eyes, touching others symbolically, which means that later they can only be used for food. By this destruction of all his material wealth, the man is considered reborn, he earns new respect and honor, and he takes a new name. As food gifts, the still living boars and the sacrificial carcasses are divided among the guests, but for every gift received, the recipient is honor-bound to repay with a boar of greater value. So as one chapter ends on the climb to power, another is just beginning.

Today on the island of Tanna, after a century of Presbyterian teaching, the people have rejected the missions, with their hospitals and schools and promises of Heaven, for they have found a new savior. He is Jon Frum, and he is on the way to Tanna.

Since 1940, Jon Frum has sent instructions, by way of a Tannese man, to reject the mission teaching, to refuse to work for the white man, to relinquish foreign money, to go back to the old ways—drink the mission-forbidden kava, dance the mission-tabooed dances—for Jon Frum said that he was coming, bringing ships full of all the desirable objects of the twentieth-century world, wonderous things to be distributed free to believers.

The cargo cult has come to Tanna. Cargo cults happen like spontaneous wildfires among peoples whose knowledge of the outside world is limited mainly to the opaque pages of the Bible. They are always led by a Christianized leader, whose Bible education and contact with foreigners, however limited, gives him the stature of a sage among his people. He mixes his new religion with the ritualistic old, and there emerges a fanatic belief in a savior who will grant everything his followers desire as soon as he learns of their needs. To contact him, his followers must perform the proper ritual. But what *is* the proper ritual? Several years ago, a New Guinea tribe tried to buy the president of the United States under the impression that this was the correct way to ensure that his foreign aid to underdeveloped countries would come their way.

On Tanna, tin cans strung by wires to towers, imitating radio transmitting stations, were the means by which Jon Frum spoke to his people. No one saw him, no one had ever seen him, he talked only to one selected Tannese who would in turn relay his messages. The authorities, in an attempt to stop the movement, arrested the leaders, who were imprisoned in the Vila jail, but the movement continued under new leaders.

With the arrival of black American soldiers in Santo and Vila during the Second World War, the Tannese saw people of their own color wearing wristwatches, driving jeeps, freely offering cigarettes. Since it was apparent that all good things had already come to black Americans, the Tannese assumed that Jon Frum must be an American and that the cargo would arrive by plane, just as it did in Vila.

No wonder, then, that Jon Frum had not yet come to Tanna! There was no airfield for his cargo planes to land. Feverishly believers tried to hack out an airstrip on their mountainous island. They made wooden images of airplanes, and from their leader they heard of daily "radio" reports of Jon Frum's imminent arrival. When an American army officer assured them that there was no Jon Frum in the United States, they refused to believe him, for after all the officer was a white man, and was it not white men who were keeping from them the cargo that was rightfully theirs?

When I was in Tanna, I climbed what has been called the "world's most accessible volcano," Mt. Yasup, marveling at the delicate pink orchids, the only vegetation growing bravely on the charcoal-colored lava slag. At the edge of the crater pit, through the stinking sulphur smoke roiling up from the thundering hellfire below, I saw a huge, faded scarlet cross erected to honor Jon Frum, as similar crosses are erected to him throughout the island. At the foot of the volcano lies the village where the late prophet, Nampas, lived with his followers. He told me that he was in regular communication with Jon Frum and that Jon Frum would be there soon. "I tell my people," he said, "we must be patient. Every day we put fresh flowers . . . by the crosses, so when he comes it will be nice." His dark eyes looked beyond me, at a vision I could not see. Was it that glorious future that enabled him and his people to endure the impoverished present? He spoke again, "You Christians—how long . . . you wait . . .for your Jesus?"

# New Caledonia

In this land there is a bird that barks but does not sing, and a fox that flies but never eats meat. Here flowers blossom without petals, and plants thrive without benefit of either roots or leaves. In this land grow the last of the planet's first seed-bearing trees, hardly changed from the time when their predecessors shaded dinosaurs some two hundred million years ago. This is the ancient land called New Caledonia.

Millions of years ago it rose much higher into the sky and was larger and a part of another land, a portion of which is now Australia. But land sank and oceans rose and the mountaintops remained as an island, long before mammals walked on earth. So the island had none until later, when the flying fox came, crossing the sea on membrane wings to feast on strange fruits growing in secret valleys. His descendants are here still, giant fruit-eating bats that are considered a gourmet delicacy by New Caledonians. The bird that barks, the kagou, flew across the ocean too, for originally it used its wings, but after settling in its adopted land and finding no predators, it forgot how to fly. And this genetic forgetfulness may soon prove its doom, for today feral dogs hunt it down in the mountain wild places that it once called its own.

Instead of real petals, the flowers of the Amborella, a shrub unique to New Caledonia, are made of leaves evolving into true petals. Rare descendants of earth's first stemmed plants, sometimes called "naked plants," still grow on the island. One species of these primitive spore-bearing survivors embeds its stems into furry trunks of tree ferns, while another has evolved enough to stand upright among moldering leaves in rocky crevices. Neither has true leaves, but rather green flaps that enable the plant to take nourishment from sun and rain. Indigenous to the island is the *niaouli*, a rather scrawny tree with a ghostly gray trunk and splayed clumps of delicate leaves. But it is the hundred-foot-tall "pine" trees that make New Caledonia and its adjacent islands so distinctive, so different appearing from other Pacific islands with their petticoat ruffles of palm trees. Little altered since their origins in the Carboniferous and Permian periods, the conifers (of the species *Araucaria*) were the first seed-bearing plants on earth—fossils that go right on living. At one time, many species blanketed almost all the world's land surfaces, but now there are only sixteen species left—and New Caledonia, with its offshore islets, claims half of them.

Tontouta, the international airport, is a drive of thirty eye-filling miles from Nouméa through gently rolling, grassy hills that rise on one side in succeeding grades toward towering spines of mountains with peaks over five thousand feet high. This Chaîne Centrale divides the long, narrow island (250 miles by 31) in two—the dry side (where the capital, Nouméa, is) and the opposite, north-eastern wet side, lush with the usual coconut palms and heavy tropical growth.

And everywhere, flawing the dark mountain flanks, gape the ugly red scars of the nickel mines, for beneath the island's skin lie vast mineral treasures—not only of nickel, but also of chromium, iron, manganese, cobalt, mercury, copper, silver, lead, coal, and even gold. Recently there has also been some oil exploration. The Société de Nickel once held a monopoly on ore processing, but lately other companies have come in, and Nouméa now is more like a boomtown than the drowsy transplant from the French Riviera that it once was. At the edge of the city, every day a flag of smoke billows in the trade winds—the nickel refinery never lets Nouméans forget that New Caledonia is a mineral treasure-trove, the richest island in Oceania. Over thirty of its residents are rumored to be millionaires.

Nouméa is not only the seat of the governor of the Territory of New Caledonia, who is also high commissioner for France in the Pacific, but it is one of the most sophisticated towns in Oceania. From the harbor to the hills, the prosperous streets are laid out in neat right angles and boast several air-conditioned hotels, a wide variety of restaurants, Paris style boutiques offering next summer's fashions (flown in weekly), and supermarkets selling gourmet foods from all over the world at shockingly high prices. Since the island does not grow enough to feed its ninety thousand inhabitants (over half of whom live in Nouméa), food must be brought in, and there is a stiff duty on all imports. Wages are high, however, and New Caledonia manages to get along without an income tax, although it does have a tax that takes a good-sized bite out of the worker's take-home pay to finance a comprehensive social service system.

Beaches and yacht harbors scallop the shores of the island from Nouméa almost to the southeast tip. It is here that New Caledonia's second largest source of income is found, for the number of tourists eager for a taste of Gallic tropic island life is steadily increasing.

Appropriately enough, it was a Frenchman, Bougainville, who first sighted the islands of New Caledonia in 1768, but it was an Englishman, Captain Cook, who first explored them a few years later. Like a homesick boy, he carved his name and the date, September 4, 1774, on one of the evergreen trees, which reminded him so much of Scotland's hills that he christened the island New Caledonia. When he tried to sail west around the island, he came to a great barrier reef, second only to Australia's in size, which caused him to retrace his passage and sail south. It was thus he discovered and named the tiny Isle of Pines, just thirty miles from the tip of Grand Terre, as the main island is sometimes called. Popular these days as a tourist paradise, with sands as fine and white as talc (which is what the sands really are), the Isle of Pines was once a dreaded name to Frenchmen. Now only moss-covered ruins threaded through with jungly roots remain to tell the story of the prison cubicles and stone walls where some of France's forty thousand political prisoners and convicts were kept during the years from 1864 to 1904, when the islands were a penal colony.

It was the government's desire to find a remote place to stash away its domestic enemies, plus the fact that French missionaries were being killed and eaten with discouraging avidity by the islanders, climaxed by word of a hearty meal composed of all the members of a French survey crew, that prompted France to annex the Territory of New Caledonia, which consisted of Grande Terre, the Isle of Pines, the three Loyalty Islands (sixty miles to the east), and the Huon Islands, an assortment of miscellaneous islets on the north. In 1853, the French raised the Tricolor practically under the nose of a British warship with annexation plans of its own; the despondent British commander committed suicide.

By then the original population of fifty to seventy thousand Melanesians had been greatly reduced, chiefly as a result of the usual diseases imported by missionaries (who first came in 1840), explorers, traders, and escaped convicts. Against these intruders the islanders defended themselves fiercely, for long practice in intervillage skirmishes had made them skilled fighters, but their simple weapons were no match for Europeans' guns and bullets. Some tribes were cannibals, and it was chiefly these who gave the islands their savage reputation.

As in other areas of Melanesia, the people were an ethnic mixture—some islanders showed definite Polynesian charactistics, others had the heavy browridge of the Australian Aborigines. About twenty different languages were spoken, but one quality most of the people had in common was that they were basically agriculturists rather than fishermen. Even today hillsides show the marks of ancient terracing and complex irrigation systems that once brought water to taro fields, usually a lowland plant. Carbon-dating of potsherds indicates that people were living in New Caledonia as far back as 1215 B.C., and successive dates prove continual residence.

As French colonists began arriving in ever greater numbers and appropriating ever more tribal land, the islanders increased their resistance, and in 1878 they embarked upon a series of massacres intended to wipe out entire colonial settlements and military encampments. At first, it almost seemed as though the *indigènes*—as the French call them—were going to be successful in their attempts to drive the intruders away, but French military might prevailed, and eventually a sort of peace descended on the territory. Now most Melanesians live on reserves on the far, "wet" side of Grande Terre. All French citizens now, they constitute a majority in the Territorial Assembly—but the assembly wields no final power.

With most Melanesians confirmed farmers and with transport of convicted persons at an end and exprisoners freed, the French soon found that they would have to import workers for mining operations and also to serve as cowhands on the big ranches, as lumberjacks in the mountain forests, and as house servants. This employers did, and from Japan, India, China, but mainly from Vietnam came contract laborers in considerable numbers. Then, during the Second World War, the United States military virtually took over New Caledonia, making decisions with scarcely even a nod to French officials, moving thousands of Japanese workers to Australia for internment, and offering far higher wages than the French. The obvious result was that imported laborers preferred working for the Americans, and after a series of unheeded uprisings, they resorted to strikes. The French promptly jailed the leaders and ordered the rest back to work under martial law.

By mid 1945, when the Pacific War ended, the New Caledonian economy was beginning to restabilize itself. Modernization of mining and refining processes eliminated some of the need for hand labor, but with expanded operations, more mine workers were still needed. Today Tahitians and Wallis Islanders, immigrants from other French colonies in the Pacific, have come to fill the gap. Since they demanded improved living accommodations, housing projects have begun to encircle Nouméa and to crawl up into the hills. Everywhere echoes the sound of hammer and saw; more and more ore-laden trucks grind their noisy way to the refineries; careening sports cars screech around mountain curves. Lost in the tumult of "progress" is the bark of the bird that has forgotten how to fly.

# Fiji

Once again the Fiji Islands are independent. For ninety-six years, the islands had worn the yoke of colonialism as a British Crown Colony. With significance the Fijians selected October 10, 1970, as their independance date—it had been October 10, 1874, when the joint chiefs of Fiji had handed a deed of cession to a representative of the British government. And Paramount Chief Cakobau had sent to Queen Victoria his most prized possession, his great war club, insignia of his power.

Over a half a century later when King George V found it in a forgotten corner of Windsor Castle, he returned it to Fiji, where, in 1931, it became the mace for the Legislative Council. Formerly used by Chief Cakobau as a head-basher for cannibal victims, it took its place in a new role as a peaceful symbol of authority, just as the Fijians themselves have changed within three generations from a life-style of Stone Age savagery to jet age sophistication. Yet they have kept many of their old proud ways.

In times past no Fijian owned personal property, for custom decreed that all he possessed was equally a possession of any of his kin. A relative might help himself to whatever he fancied without a murmur of please or thanks. The custom, called *kerekere*, has long been outlawed by authorities, but it continues to this day to flourish underground. While Fijians are reluctant to work for wages alone, they are willing to labor long and hard for the causes of duty, tradition, or loyalty.

The Fiji archipelago, large in number of islands but small in ocean area (325 by 225 miles) has been a crossroads of Pacific travel since long before the recent tourist boom. A thousand years ago Polynesians migrating eastward stopped at Fiji on their way toward Tonga, 180 miles to the southeast, or Samoa, northeast by 500 miles. Rotuma and its isles, about two hundred miles northwest of Fiji, are also Polynesian.

Except for a few atolls, the islands of Fiji are high and of volcanic origin, some with an admixture of limestone uplifts. Geologists believe that the islands were once part of a continental shelf extending as far as the Philippines and Australia. Of Fiji's 361 islands, only thirty are more than five square miles in size and only one hundred are inhabited.

The chain of some twenty tiny Yasawa Islands shapes the western edge of Fiji, while at the eastern boundary lie the fifty-seven islets of the Lau Group. Between these two island flanks is the heart of Fiji—its three largest islands, Viti Levu, Vanua Levu, and Taveuni. Taveuni is by far the smallest, but it is famous for its picturesque beauty and the fertility of its soil. Only a few miles off the coast of Vanua Levu, it is crossed by the 180° meridian (the International Dateline), which led to some lively times in the days when missionaries held the power to prevent people from working on Sunday. One merchant built a store directly on the line, half on one side, half on the other. He could conduct business on the east side through Saturday; then, by opening the west door, he could continue operating the following day, which was technically still Saturday. In 1879, the line was jogged so that all the Fiji Islands, as well as neighboring Tonga, are in the same time zone.

The largest and most popular island, Viti Levu, is oval in shape with high, verdant interior mountains that bring tropical downpours regularly to one side of the island and restrict the rainfall on the other side. Suva, the capital since 1882, lies on the wet southeast coast, while Nadi, the site of the international airport, is on the opposite, dry side. European explorers trying to capture phonetically the sound of Viti, marked their maps with such attempts as: Beetee, Fegee, Fijee, Feegee, Fidge, Fidschi, Feigee, Viji, Vitee, and of course, Fiji, which became the collective name for all the islands.

According to radiocarbon dating of artifacts, people were living on Viti Levu over five hundred years before the birth of Christ. Since both Samoa and Tonga were settled later, their future Polynesian residents, sailing from Malay-Indonesia, presumably used Fiji as their last port of call. There they acquired a pottery skill whose Melanesian origin can be traced, in both technique and design, from New Caledonia to Fiji, then to Tonga, Samoa, and the Marquesas.

Fijian legend credits a huge snake god named Degei with the creation of life from two eggs that he hatched. From them emerged the first man and the first woman, the ancestors of all Fijians. Degei taught them how to grow yams and bananas and how to make fire, and he sent his son, Rokomoutu, to scoop up the islands from the ocean floor and shape them and place them on the surface of the water so the Fijians might have a place to live. Where Rokomoutu's tapa robes trailed upon the land, sandy beaches appeared; when he lifted his robe, there rose rocky cliffs.

Degei slept in a cave, and when he was awakened each morning by a dove, he would cause night to vanish and daylight to appear. This custom infuriated his nephews, who were boatbuilders, because they wanted to sleep longer, so they killed the dove. In revenge, Degei caused a flood to sweep the boatbuilder clan apart and set them on different islands of Fiji, where they were to be servants forever to the chiefs.

It was the skill of the Lau Islands' boatbuilders that cemented the relationship between Fijians and Tongans. Tongans desired the great one-hundred-foot-long vessels that could carry as many as two hundred men. As payment for these *druas*, the Tongans offered warriors to the chiefs to help in their continual cannibal wars with neighboring islands. By the end of the nineteenth century, the influence of more sophisticated Western ships had made the building of *druas* an obsolete skill.

Abel Tasman of Holland (who later left his name to an island and a sea off Australia) is credited with being the first European to sail in Fijian waters and to live to tell of it. This happened in 1643, and Tasman's stories of his experiences with the treacherous northern reefs of Fiji and the fierce, man-eating Fijians were such that navigators steered clear of the whole area for the next 130 years. Even Captain Cook contented himself with a brief survey of the southern islands in 1774, while Captain Bligh's account fifteen years later of his escape from pursuing cannibals in the Yasawas only added to Fiji's unsavory reputation. It was not until 1840 that an expedition headed by Commander Wilkes of the United States Navy correctly charted Fiji's many islands.

A few white men, however, had settled in Fiji as early as 1804—mostly escaped convicts from Australia and such beachcombers as Charlie Savage, known as the "terrible Swede"—a man who changed the history of Fiji. Having jumped ship in Tonga, he got a ride on the American brig *Eliza*, carrying sandalwood, but the *Eliza* cracked up on a Fijian reef. Savage survived, along with a load of guns and ammunition. Savage's great weakness was women—and his great strength was a shrewd eye. To the chief of tiny Bau Island he offered an exchange, guns for women. In return for an unlimited supply of the latter, Savage became a mercenary soldier in the service of the chief, neatly pointing out that only white men were capable of firing guns.

However, other white outlaws joined forces with enemy chiefs, and for the next half century the islands of Fiji reverberated with the blast of gunfire, while village cooking pits were seldom cool. In 1813 Savage was clubbed and duly eaten, but by that time Bau warriors, having learned that guns knew no color, were themselves good shots, and Bau had become the dominant force in western Fiji.

Bau, joined to Viti Levu by a short causeway, was important not for its size, which is only twenty acres, but for its chiefs, in particular, Cakobau, who eventually became paramount chief of the western islands, in short, "king" of Fiji. Even today most of Fiji's highest ranking chiefs come from Bau, although most of them now work in government administration on other islands. The language spoken originally on Bau has become standard Fijian and is used throughout the islands, while written Fijian, composed by some well-meaning missionaries, trips many a visitor's tongue and affords utter confusion between the spoken and printed word. Nadi, for example, is prounced Nandi—it has a hidden "n" sound that accompanies the letter "d." There are more complications: "b" is really "mb"; "g" is "ng" (as in singer); "q" is "ng-g" (as in finger); and "c" is pronounced like "th" in the. So Cakobau's name is actually pronounced Thakombau.

A small offshore island near Suva, Beqa, is pronounced Mbengga, but that is not the reason for its fame—the men of Beqa-Mbengga can walk unharmed across the white-hot stones of a fire pit. Legend recounts how they gained this unusual ability. Long ago there lived on the island a chief, Tui N'Kualita, who one morning went to a mountain stream to catch an eel, a promised gift for a storyteller in his village. When caught, however, the eel turned into a tiny spirit-man, who, in return for his freedom, offered to make Tui N'Kualita the greatest warrior of Beqa. "But I am already the greatest warrior of Beqa," said the chief. Then the little spirit promised overwhelming success in love. "But I already have all the wives I want," countered the chief, picking up the little man and remarking what a great delicacy he would be for the storyteller. Now desperate, the spirit offered to show the chief how to live in a fire pit for four days and emerge unscathed. But Tui N'Kualita had no desire to waste four days in a cooking pit nor any great trust in the little man's motives. As a final bribe, the tiny spirit said he would teach Tui N'Kualita how to walk on hot stones, and the chief agreed that was worth knowing. Once he had learned the ritual, he freed the spirit-man and then taught the skill to the men of Beqa, who are still famous today for this accomplishment.

By the mid 1800s, foreign settlers had moved in and had begun planting cotton on the island of Ovalau, ten miles off the coast of Viti Levu, but many of the islanders, especially the mountain tribesmen, were antagonistic and gave vent to their animosity by raiding foreign settlements. As a result, some of the American planters filed claims for damages against the "king" of Fiji, Cakobau of Bau; and then, when the American consul somehow managed to burn down his consulate while celebrating the Fourth of July, he also blamed Cakobau and filed another suit for damages. Altogether, the claims amounted to nearly fifty thousand dollars.

But the "king" had no hard cash and apparently no way of getting any. In the economy of Fiji, wealth and power had always been measured by food and war captives. But the Americans wanted ready money and they kept sending warships to Fiji to back up their claim. Desparate, Cakobau, in 1858, offered Fiji to Great Britain if only Britain would pay the so-called debt and get the United States off his back. London considered the matter for two years but finally refused. Cakobau then approached Washington, but President Lincoln, busy with other matters in 1861, did not even answer the paramount chief's offer. A decade later, even the empire-builder of the Pacific, Germany, refused to accept a gift of the Fiji Islands. Nobody, it seemed, wanted the infamous "cannibal isles."

Nor was the American "debt" Cakobau's only problem. Ma'afu, Tongan chief of the Lau Islands and his missionary friends kept fussing at him to repent of his savage and heathen ways and put an end to cannibalism. In 1867 came the culminating incident. A hill tribe on Viti Levu ate the Reverend Thomas Baker, boots and all. Cakobau protested that it was the missionary's own fault, for he had touched the head of the tribal chief while trying to present him with a gift of a comb—and that, by Fijian custom, was the ultimate insult and could only be answered by instant death. But the only interest missionaries took in local customs was an ardent desire to see them banished as soon as possible. Cakobau's explanation was unacceptable, and as pressure increased he was forced to embrace Christianity. The Reverend

Thomas Baker retains the distinction of being the last missionary to be eaten in Fiji, and today the Fijians are one hundred percent Christian.

In 1873 the beset but newly christianized Cakobau approached England again, and London, reluctantly, acceded, and with the Deed of Cession endorsed by Cakobau, Ma'afu, and eleven other chiefs, the Fiji Islands became a Crown Colony.

In 1879, the European settlers imported the first laborers from India to work the sugarcane fields, for this was work that Fijians refused to do. Thirty-seven years later, when the custom was stopped, forty thousand Indians chose to stay on—and now there are more Indians in Fiji than Fijians.

But it is the Indians who not only provide most of the labor in sugarcane production, Fiji's number-one export, but also dominate town life. They are teachers, doctors, lawyers, politicians, store owners, office workers, and taxi drivers. But they cannot buy land.

Most Fijians, on the other hand, still prefer to live as they always have, in small villages under the guidance of a chief, leading a shared subsistence agricultural life that provides basic needs for all village members. Under the Native Land Trust, over three million acres belong to more than sixty-five hundred land-holding tribal units. About four hundred thousand acres of land are freehold and can be bought and sold, but prices are greatly inflated now that tourist developments are passing gold, and copra is challenging sugar as Fiji's most important money-maker. Government lands of over three hundred thousand acres cannot be sold, only leased.

Land may become a Pandora's box for newly independent Fiji.

New Guinea

Preceding page: Purari River, Southern Highlands.
Above: On the road to Mt. Hagen.
Right: Western Highlands.
Far right: Man from the Western Highlands.

34

Below: Preparing for a sing-sing, Mt. Hagen area.
Right: Enga people, Western Highlands.

Below: Decoration for a sing-sing, Mt. Hagen.
Right: Kukukuku men from the Eastern Highlands.
Opposite: Chimbu people, Western Highlands.

Above: Highlands man masked for a dance.
Right and opposite: Mudmen of the Asaro Valley, Eastern Highlands.

Opposite: Western Highlands warriors prepare for battle.
Below: Patrol headed for the Jimi River area, Western
Highlands.

Above: Danny Leahy, pioneer explorer and gold prospector.

Right above: Father Ross, pioneer missionary.

Right below: Jack Fox, pioneer explorer and gold prospector.

Opposite left: Woman, Western Highlands.

Opposite right: Country boys, Western Highlands.

44

Below: Highlands men cooking yams.
Opposite: Slash and burn agriculture, Western Highlands.

47

Below: Red-plumed bird of paradise.
Right: King of Saxony bird of paradise.
Right below: Hair-crested bird of paradise.
Opposite above: Ribbon-tailed bird of paradise.
Opposite below left: Victoria crested pigeon.
Opposite below right: New Guinea hornbill.

# New Hebrides

Opposite: Mt. Yasur, an active volcano, Tanna.
Right: Small Nambas dancer, Malekula.

Above: Bark-masked dancer, Malekula.
Right: Small Nambas dancers, Malekula.
Opposite: Fanla Village dancers before a
slit log drum, Ambrym.

Above: Ambrym warrior.
Right: Chief Tofor of Fanla Village, Ambrym.
Opposite: Prince Philip, Duke of Edinburgh, visits Vila, Efate.

54

Above: Copra production, Malekula.
Right: Father and son, Malekula.
Opposite: A Tanna girl combs her hair.

56

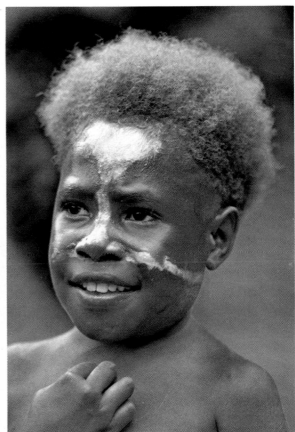

Left: Hanging a grass skirt out to dry, Tanna.
Above: Tanna boy ready for circumcision ceremony.
Opposite: Children of Sulphur Bay Village herd goats on
Mt. Yasur lava flow.

Above: Nampas, late leader of the Jon Frum Society, Tanna.

Left: Wooden cross of the Jon Frum Society, Tanna.

Opposite left: A young girl after communion, Vila, Efate.

Opposite right: Local market, Vila, Efate.

Left: Carved mask of a slit log drum.

Below: Wooden figure from island legend, Ambrym.

Bottom: Slit log drum, Fanla Village, Ambrym.

Opposite left: Carved figures indicating social rank stand beside houses.

Opposite right above: A painted mask to help yam vines grow.

Opposite right below: Human skulls covered with vegetable paste.

Opposite: Lagoon and reefs near Isle of Pines.
Left: Net fisherman, Ouvéa, Loyalty Islands.
Above: Pacific green turtle, Isle of Pines.

65

Above: Open cut nickel mine, New Caledonia.

Far left: Smelter worker, Nouméa.

Left: Smelter of the French-owned Société de Nickel, Nouméa.

Opposite: Nouméa, often called "Paris of the Pacific."

Above and opposite: Children of the Isle of Pines.

Right, below, and opposite: Dancers, Isle of Pines.

Left: "Sea Eagles," Mouly Atoll, Loyalty Islands.
Below: "Sea Eagle" catch, Mouly Atoll.
Opposite above: Melanesian cattleman.
Opposite below: Cattle drive, New Caledonia.

Above: Isle of Pines.
Opposite above: "Sisters," Ouvéa Atoll, Loyalty Islands.
Opposite left: Restaurant workers, Ouvéa.
Opposite right: French military parade, Nouméa.

Below: Petroglyph.
Right: A kagou, the bird that barks, New Caledonia.
Opposite left: Sunset, New Caledonia.
Opposite right: Watching a cricket game, Nouméa.

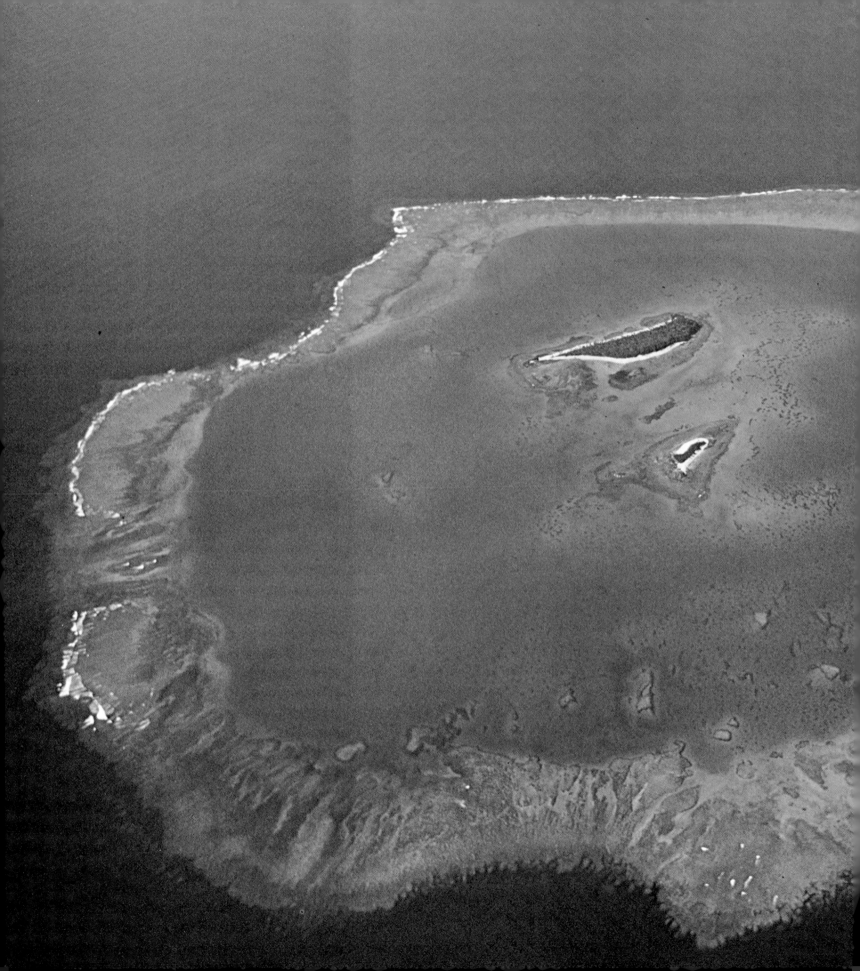

# Fiji

Atoll, Lau Islands.

Below: Fijian, Viti Levu.
Right: Providing song and music for a dance, Viti Levu.
Opposite: Fijian dancers, Viti Levu.

Above and right: Indian Hindu ceremony, Viti Levu.
Opposite: Indian Hindu wedding ceremony, Viti Levu.

84

Below: Rainstorm over Suva Harbor, Viti Levu.
Opposite left: Mussels, Suva market.
Opposite right above: Suva policeman wearing traditional *sulu*.
Opposite right below: Suva market.

Right: Ratu George Cakobau (Thakombau),
great-grandson of the "king" of Fiji.
Opposite: Fire walkers from Beqa Island.

Opposite: Transporting sugarcane near Nandi, Viti Levu.
Above: Gold ore, Vatukoula, Viti Levu.
Right: One week's gold output, Emperor Gold Mines, Viti Levu.
Overleaf: Taveuni scene.

# Micronesia

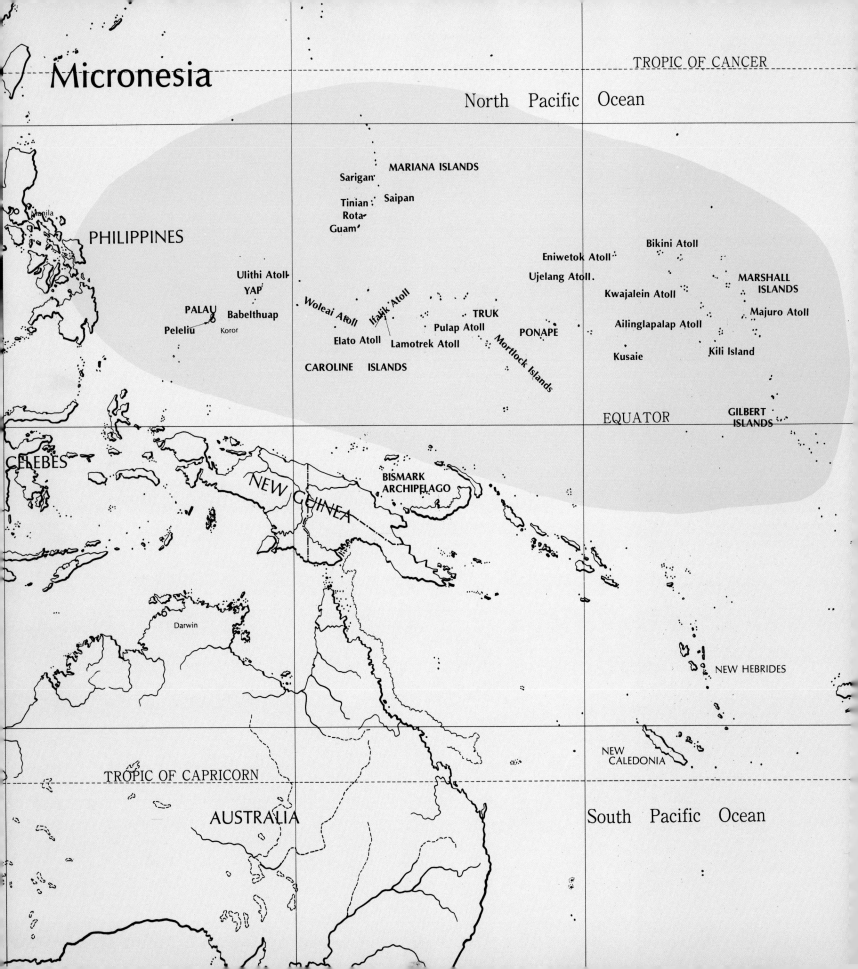

# Micronesia

TROPIC OF CANCER

North Pacific Ocean

PHILIPPINES

Manila

**MARIANA ISLANDS**

Sarigan

Tinian · Saipan

Rota

Guam

Bikini Atoll

Eniwetok Atoll

Ujelang Atoll.

**MARSHALL ISLANDS**

Ulithi Atoll

**YAP**

**PALAU** Babelthuap

Peleliu Koror

Woleai Atoll

Ifalik Atoll

Elato Atoll

Lamotrek Atoll

**TRUK**

Pulap Atoll

Mortlock Islands

**PONAPE**

Kwajalein Atoll

Ailinglapalap Atoll

Majuro Atoll

Kili Island

Kusaie

**CAROLINE ISLANDS**

CELEBES

**NEW GUINEA**

**BISMARK ARCHIPELAGO**

EQUATOR

**GILBERT ISLANDS**

Darwin

NEW HEBRIDES

NEW CALEDONIA

TROPIC OF CAPRICORN

**AUSTRALIA**

South Pacific Ocean

# Micronesia

Across the tropical northwestern Pacific's ocean wilderness are scattered the divergent islands and atolls for which there is no better name than Micronesia—"Small Islands." Their ocean space is often equated with the area of the continental United States (some three million square miles). Yet within that watery vastness, the total land area of Micronesia is an inconstant 711 miles, the exact figure depending on the land-eating sea action of the latest typhoon. The islands themselves range from cartoon-image, one-palm deserted islets, to gently rolling lands, to towering volcanic isles of startling beauty.

In any case, the contrast is not easy to visualize. But try this: take the tiny state of Rhode Island and divide it roughly into two; then crumble the larger half into 2,203 fragments of varying sizes and shapes and sprinkle them haphazardly over those three million square miles. Then bear in mind that out of those two-thousand-odd small islands and atolls, fewer than one hundred are large and fertile enough for human habitation. Some of the atolls support as few as eight people; large volcanic islands, over ten thousand; in all, there are fewer than one hundred thousand Micronesians.

Geographically Micronesia is divided into three main archipelagos: the volcanic Marianas, the Carolines, and the coral Marshalls. Administratively Micronesia (excepting the British-ruled subequatorial Gilberts) is now known as the United States Trust Territory of the Pacific Islands.

But this is only the latest era in the history of the Micronesians, who, since the earliest foreign discoveries, have played the role of political pawns, while their islands became prizes in chess games between warring alien nations, each attempting to checkmate enemies unknown to the Micronesians.

Guam it where is started, this foreign plunder of the Pacific. The date was March 6, 1521, when the Portuguese navigator, Ferdinand Magellan, sailing under the flag of Spain, stopped there on his astonishing attempt to circumnavigate the globe—astonishing, at least on the Pacific part of the voyage, because he sailed ninety-eight days from the tip of South America, all the way across the isle-freckled South Pacific and then north of the equator, without making a landfall until he reached Guam's southwestern coast. Inevitably he was a bit touchy after being cooped up so long with a starving and mutinous crew; thus, when friendly Chamorros paddled toward his ship with welcome canoeloads of food, Magellan ordered his men to shoot, killing several of the islanders and setting a precedent for the centuries of Spanish rule that were to follow.

Some two centuries after the arrival of the first missionaries (1668), Spanish hegemony in Micronesia was challenged by Germany's expanding Pacific empire, which in 1885 laid claim to the Marshalls and to Spanish-claimed islands in the western Carolines. The Spaniards requested the mediation of the Pope, who ruled in favor of Spanish ownership but granted free trading rights to all countries. In 1899, Spain, impoverished by the Spanish-American War, sold its Micronesian claims to Germany for about four million dollars. Guam had already become a possession of the United States the previous year as a result of the Treaty of Paris.

With the outbreak of the First World War in 1914, Japan, as England's ally, moved into Micronesia. The Japanese took possession of all German-owned islands wholly north of the equator, which (save for the British Gilberts) neatly encompassed all of Micronesia as well as two Polynesian inhabited atolls. When in 1920 the League of Nations mandated the islands to the imperial government, the Japanese settled in with permanent intentions, planting vast sugarcane fields, introducing new farm produce, mining phosphate, and establishing fish processing plants for use by their far-ranging fleets.

After 1935, when Japan left the League, they prohibited all foreign travel through the islands. The reason for this imposed secrecy became apparent several years later. Micronesia had become a vast complex of naval and air bases of enormous strategic importance, as the United States discovered somewhat tardily on December 7, 1941. The war was not kind to Micronesia, nor was the immediate aftermath, when for six years the islands were administered by the United States Navy. Having been granted the right to fortify them, the navy promptly proceeded to do so, closing the territory to all casual travelers. In 1951, most of the islands—save for the Marianas and Bikini, Eniwetok, and Kwajalein atolls in the Marshalls—were transferred to administration by the Department of the Interior. Finally, in 1962, the Marianas were joined to the trust territory. Under the unique provisions of a United Nations mandate, the United States governs the islands as a strategic trust territory; thus, it has the power, after Security Council agreement, to close off the entire territory or any part of it for reasons of military security.

Today the trust territory is administered from headquarters on Saipan by a high commission, headed by a high commissioner, a political appointee of the president of the United States. Under him are six district administrators, one for each district into which the trust territory is now divided—Palau, Yap, Truk, Ponape, the Marshall Islands, and the Mariana Islands. Each district has a local congress and also elects representatives to the Congress of Micronesia, a bicameral house created in 1962. The Congress's resolutions must be submitted to the high commissioner, who (under the Secretary of the Interior in Washington) possesses the power of veto.

Where did they come from, these people whose lives have been shaped by the islands they chose? They started from that launching place of most Pacific islanders, the Malay Peninsula. They blended the physical traits of Mongoloid, Caucasoid, and Negroid races that they met long ago during their slow, island-hopping Pacific treks.

Unlike their predecessors, the Papuans and Melanesians who settled the "Black Islands," the Austronesians, as they have been named, were accomplished seamen and navigators, and with their well-designed oceangoing canoes, they pushed east and north into unknown seas toward the "Small Islands." The most recent carbon dating of artifacts establishes settlements in the Marianas as early as 1500 B.C.

Micronesians really have little more in common than their imposed name. Languages and customs differ so much that ethnographers divide the peoples of the trust territory into nine main groups—Palauans, Trukese, Ponapeans, Kusaieans, Polynesians, Yapese, Marshallese, Chamorro, and the atoll dwellers of the Carolines. The islanders, however, make further distinctions, calling themselves after whichever of the ninety-six bits of Micronesian land they call home. This diversity of languages, traditions, and loyalties makes cohesive action difficult for the Congress of Micronesia, whose members sometimes must revert to Japanese in order to communicate with each other.

The flora of Micronesia was carried there in part by wind or waves or far-flying birds, but most of it was brought by man himself, as was the island fauna (with the exception of four varieties of bats). A contribution of the Spaniards was *Rattus rattus*, the European black rat, which scuttled ashore from the first galleons to call at the Marianas. The rat suddenly found he had never had it so good: the year-round warm climate was ideal, food was plentiful, and there were no natural enemies. Since under such ideal conditions one pair of affectionate rats can produce twenty million descendants in three years of life, the islanders soon found themselves on the point of being driven from their own land by this foreign pest.

In an effort to keep the rat population down, the Spanish brought in a quantity of monitor lizards, known for their predilection for rat flesh. The outcome might have been predicted—there was soon a lizard population explosion. To combat it, the desperate colonists now imported a poisonous toad, which the gullible lizards also found to their liking. As a result, the islanders now seldom encounter a lizard, but the poisonous toad population poses a serious threat to domestic animals—while the rat continues to live its furtive, and all too fertile, life.

Getting away from rats, lizards, and toads, let us consider for a moment the tourist. All an American needs to enter Micronesia now is proof of citizenship; all a non-American needs is a visa. Modern hotels are springing up on all the main islands, and recently Air Micronesia's jets have established a new unity between the islands that serve as district headquarters and the outside world. Air Micronesia, incidentally, is backed by the islanders themselves as shareholders, cooperating with mainland-based Continental Airlines. The more remote atolls and islands are reachable by slow boat, and indications are that Micronesia will soon be enjoying—or any way putting up with—a tourist boom.

# Mariana Islands

Curving north above Guam for more than 350 miles are fifteen high volcanic islands that gradually diminish in size like green beads of some broken necklace. These are the Marianas.

These are "new" additions to Micronesia's minuscule islands, poking above the sea's surface only recently, as land birth is measured—about fifty or sixty million years ago, at the beginning of the present, Cenozoic, era.

They were a long time aborning. Their conception began when an upheaval of the earth's crust some ten million years before had thrust into mid-Asian skies the world's highest surviving mountains, the Himalayas. This cataclysm of the earth's surface disturbed the ocean floor at the continent's edge in the Cretaceous period, when the continent reached much further into the ocean. Terrible pressures opened fissures in the ocean bottom, permitting magma to escape. Hot liquid rock met cold sea water and caused the surrounding ocean to churn with unimaginable boiling convulsions and explosions. Oozing ever upward, this molten rock flowed for immeasurable time before it eventually appeared on the ocean's face. More epochs passed as it cooled and grew firm and disappeared under the water and then rose again and again to new heights. After ages of flirting with existence, the islands lay quiet while continual storms sculpted the lava into valleys and laced the ravines with plunging streams. Heavy rains picking at the rocks washed them bit by bit to lower levels, where, in some later time plant roots netting the soil prevented further erosion, and around the shores polyps began to build their wedding rings of coral against an unrelenting sea.

Impressed by the swift Chamorro vessels, with their great triangular sails, Ferdinand Magellan in 1521 named Guam and the adjacent islands *Las Islas de las Velas Latinas* —"The Islands of the Lateen Sails." This agreeable name, however, he all too soon altered to *Los Ladrones*, "The Thieves," for the Stone Age Chamorros, suddenly introduced to iron, were almost certainly overzealous in fulfilling their desire for the miraculous metal.

Formal annexation took place in 1565; then for more than three hundred years Guam and her archipelago were subjected to Spanish domination, from which they were never to recover. The first permanent settlers were Catholic missionaries, who, accompanied by armed guards, arrived in 1668. After changing the name of the islands to the Marianas (in honor of Queen Maria Anna), they quickly set about their business of conversion. For the next thirty years, the Chamorros were granted a simple choice: Christianity or death. Chamorro resistance to this dictate gave rise to a Spanish manhunt throughout the Marianas; its intention was to put every male Chamorro to death, and it nearly succeeded. A population once estimated at one hundred thousand had been reduced by 1790 to about sixteen hundred, most of them women and children.

Today there are no longer any pure Chamorros in the world, and their history and culture have vanished, while only a hybrid version of their language lingers on. The present-day "Chamorros" are descendants of Chamorro women who intermarried many years ago with Spanish,

Filipinos, and Mexicans—and they are all, of course, devout Catholics.

The largest and southernmost island in the archipelago, Guam, is not administratively part of the trust territory, since it became a United States possession in 1898. Some thirty miles long and varying in width from under four miles at its pinched waist to over eight miles at its widest point, Guam possesses a total area of just over two hundred square miles (one-third of which is military and off limits to civilians). Guamanians consider much of their island to be jungle (although it bears little resemblance to a true rain forest) and they like to claim Mt. Lamlam as the highest mountain in the world, although only 1,334 feet of it are visible above sea level. Its roots, however, lie 36,198 feet under water, in the earth's deepest known scar, the Mariana Trench.

The island's population of about forty thousand are American citizens, as are Guam's military personnel and their families, whose number varies between thirty and forty thousand, but most of the tourists at present are Japanese. Less than fifteen hundred miles from Tokyo by plane, Guam has become so popular with Japanese brides and grooms that it is frequently included in a package deal comprising a wedding ceremony and a reception in Japan and then a honeymoon on a tropic beach. Couples with wedding checks to spend are pleased to discover that among Guam's numerous attractions are the duty-free shops of Agana. Recently it has built several new hotels to attract more tourists (as well as more investors) from the United States, using as its slogan "Guam—Where America's Day Begins." Actually, it is where America's tomorrow begins, for Guam, some five thousand miles west of San Francisco, lies on the other side of the International Dateline (as

does all the trust territory; however, "strategic," military-occupied Kwajalein is tied to Honolulu time).

Just to the north of Guam rise Rota, Tinian, and Saipan, the largest in the chain after Guam, although five other Marianas are big and fertile enough to support human life. One—Sarigan—boasts a community of some twenty souls. The total land area of the Marianas (excluding Guam) is only 183 square miles, and the total population is just a little more than ten thousand.

Rota, only twelve miles by five and one-half, with a population of a little over one thousand, has been converted into one large truck garden to help feed Guam's hungry inhabitants and visitors. The Chamorro spoken by the people of Rota is said to be the purest in the Marianas, the reason being that during the Spanish religious purges some of Rota's Chamorros succeeded in concealing themselves in caves and so escaped death or expatriation.

A quarter of tiny Tinian (only ten miles by four and one-half) has been leased as a cattle ranch, and now fat Black Angus cattle placidly graze near overgrown runways from which—on August 6, 1945—the B-29 bomber *Enola Gay* headed north for Hiroshima; three days later another set out for Nagasaki. Today plaques mark the sites where the atomic bombs were loaded. Remains of other memorials—left by another people—stand nearby. Called *latte* stones, these are double rows of six-foot-high pillars topped by great reverse-dome caps. They were built in an unknown age, for an unknown purpose, by an unknown tribe, who, perhaps, lived in a gentler time. Saipan, fourteen miles long, is the largest island in the Mariana archipelago besides Guam. Though largely depopulated by the Spanish religious purges, a few islanders had returned by the time the Germans took over. The latter founded the port town of Garapan, from where they hoped to carry off great boatloads of copra. The Germans' successors, the Japanese, exterminated the aging coconut palms and planted sugarcane instead (as they had on both Rota and Tinian), at the same time greatly enlarging the town. At the height of Japanese activity, there were six sugar mills employing forty thousand people. Most of the labor was imported, but some of the benefits of this booming enterprise brushed off, to contribute to the prosperity of the few islanders.

During the war, a month's desperate fighting took 3,144 American casualties and forced the defenders to the northern cliff of the island, where over three thousand Japanese (mostly civilians) chose the 830-foot drop to the rocky shore below rather than surrender. Garapan was totally destroyed during the fighting and has never been rebuilt. The only physical remains of the last two occupations are the German lighthouse on Garapan Heights and the bullet-scarred bronze statue of the Japanese who founded Saipan's sugarcane industry.

When I arrived at Saipan's airport, shortly after Air Micronesia began scheduled flights, I was surprised to see a group of Japanese standing about in the midday tropical sun—men in dark, heavy suits, women in winter kimonos, all with fans fluttering and all carrying boxes wrapped in white cloths. The group was waiting for the continuing flight to Okinawa and then home. When I inquired, I learned that the white-wrapped boxes contained rocks. The Japanese had come, as soon as they could, to visit the death place of their relatives and, being unable to recover bones, they were taking home instead memorial rocks from Suicide Cliff.

Once a thriving Chamorro community, Saipan has seen extermination of its people, destruction of its once bountiful coconut palms, rape of the soil's fertility by sugarcane, devastation of the land by bombs, and finally, threat of disastrous erosion of the soil. It was this final menace that led the American military to sweep the entire island with planes that dropped seeds of a tenacious tropical weed, which had but one good quality—its soil-holding ability. Bushy growth now covers the interior of the island, where rusting implements of war as well as viable explosives lie hidden beneath scrub, making certain areas still off limits.

Nestling in a bowl of brilliant green, a thousand feet above the placid lagoon, are the offices and residences of trust territory personnel. Capitol Hill, as the complex is called, was built secretly in the postwar years by the navy to serve as headquarters for training Nationalist Chinese guerrilla fighters—supposedly a brainchild of the Central Intelligence Agency. In 1962, when the navy reluctantly gave up its grip on the island, the trust territory fell heir to the spread of buildings scattered over wide, well-kept lawns. It looks like a country club somewhere in America's affluent exurbia. It should; it cost the United States around thirty million dollars.

Sitting comfortably on the veranda of one of the bungalows that house trust territory employees, a cool glass in my hand, watching the evening sun perform its daily miracle on the horizon, I wondered what the Marianas would be like now if all that money had been differently spent. Thirty million dollars divided by ten thousand people. . . . But the sunset had suddenly invented some unbelievable new colors—mathematics and the CIA forgotten, I settled back to enjoy a glory of Saipan that would be with me all my life.

# Yap

In the time of long ago, as legend goes, a Yapese chief, contemplating the beauty of a full tropical moon, decided that something like the moon—round, white, beautiful, and permanent: a stone moon—would make an ideal form of money for his people.

There being no such stone on the cluster of four Yap islets, the chief, after council with ten other chiefs of Yap, sent a "moon rock" expedition out across unknown seas, for in those distant days most Yapese believed that their islands and atolls were the only lands in the world.

Nevertheless, a month later, the Yap sailors sighted Palau, some 220 miles to the southwest—but the Palauans refused to let the Yapese land to search for the desired rocks. The Yapese chiefs, accordingly, sent out a second and stronger expedition, which gave battle to the Palauans and won the right to go ashore. Failing to find stones like those the chief had described, the Yapese, instead, discovered Palau's limestone cliffs, where they cut out a large, round, flat disc of sparkling white. They chipped a hole in the center, inserted a wooden pole in order to transport the stone down to the water's edge, and, balancing it precariously on their fragile outrigger canoes, carried it home in triumph to Yap.

So began one of the most extraordinary episodes in the saga of Pacific island sailing. Ever larger and larger stones came into demand—and this presented problems not only of quarrying and land transport but also of getting these enormously heavy pieces of stone money across a sometimes rampageous Pacific in small canoes. Many were the Yapese men who lost their lives in the process.

Then, late in the nineteenth century, came an American renegade, David O'Keefe, sole survivor of the reef-wrecked *Belvidere* out of Savannah, Georgia. As he convalesced, he watched Yap's only other foreign resident, a frustrated German copra buyer, trying to force reluctant Yapese to meet copra quotas by confiscating their stone money. The importance that the islanders attached to the stones gave O'Keefe an idea. Returning to Yap a year later as captain of a Chinese junk, he offered safe transport for workers to and from Palau and bigger pieces of stone money in exchange for trepang (dried sea cucumber), a prized ingredient of Chinese soup, and copra, which he would sell in Hong Kong and Manila.

Thus it was the American captain of a Chinese junk who brought to Yap its largest piece of money (which is now on the islet of Rumung); it measures twelve by ten feet, is one and one-half feet thick, and weighs almost five tons. Yapese know the history and age of each piece of stone money, which, in addition to color, quality, and shape, determines final value. Therefore, the older pieces of money are considered of greater value than the more easily obtained O'Keefe money.

In 1929, the Japanese counted 13,281 pieces of stone money, but during the war many were crushed to build roads and others were carried away to be used as anchors. Since the Germans outlawed the quarrying of the money, the pieces that have survived have increased in value. They are still a useful medium of exchange. Shortly before my first visit to Yap, I learned that one village had purchased land from another and paid for it with stone money. The money itself remains where it is; only the title changes. Stone money is both permanent and decorative and has the added advantage of requiring no armed men to guard it.

Stone money is the proper medium of exchange for an elaborate intervillage celebration called a *mitmit*, which may last a month and cost a host village the equivalent of six thousand dollars in stone money. The greatest cost of a *mitmit* occurs during a special song and dance routine when any girl or woman is supposed to be granted whatever her heart desires, a tradition that sometimes cleans out Colonia's trade stores. The host village, incidentally, recovers the same stone money in some later year, when the guest village returns the festival.

Colonia, Yap's only town, is the district headquarters for an area stretching over 700 miles eastward and 460 miles north to Guam. The smallest trust territory district in both land area and population (once estimated at fifty thousand; now about sixty-eight hundred), the inhabitants live mostly on Yap proper, with only about twenty-five hundred atoll dwellers on the nine inhabited atolls. Yap itself comprises four main islands separated only by narrow saltwater channels, all within a fringing reef.

The atolls in the Yap District are a different story. Basically atolls form when the island within a reef sinks beneath the sea, leaving, like a memorial wreath, a stony ring of coral. Eventually, through the work of wind, waves, and weather, drifts of coral sand collect and vegetation grows. These, then, are the homes of the Pacific atoll dwellers.

The whole archipelago of the Carolines, which includes the present districts of Yap, Palau, Truk, and Ponape, were explored and named by the Spanish in honor of King Charles II of Spain. They annexed it then forgot it, turning instead to the Marianas to the north, until the Germans and David O'Keefe reminded them that the Carolines were still there.

If foreign invaders have been a trial to the Yapese, the Yapese have been a trial to the foreigners who came hoping to change their ways. Spain brought them its particular brand of Catholicism, while Germany countered with Lutheran Protestantism, and now about ninety percent of the Yapese profess Christianity—while the *tamerongs*, or magician-seers, practice quietly, and whispers of sorcery surround disasters. And Yapese continue to wear the clothes they have always worn.

A woman's everyday ankle-length skirt, made of a combination of palm fronds, ferns, and grasses, takes two days to make and lasts about two weeks; then it is thrown away and a new one made. A cloth dress, on the other hand, not only costs money and has to be washed now and then, but also endangers exposing the wearer's thighs (shocking to Yapese). Besides, fabric is hot, confining, and not nearly so provocative as a rustling grass skirt. A simple, traditional slender black cord—symbol of womanhood—hung around her neck completes a Yapese lady's costume.

In the early days of the trusteeship, the wife of an American administrator insisted that her husband "do something" about those exposed bosoms, so he issued T-shirts to the women with instructions to wear them when in town. The women obeyed—after having cut suitable holes in their shirts to nurse their babies.

The loincloth—called a *thu*—is the Yapese symbol of manhood. Every boy is taught by the time he is one year old, how to wear it and as he grows older he adds more fabric, usually of different colors. When he reaches manhood, he adds on top of the cloths a *kafar*, strands of dried hibiscus tree bark. On the first day that he appears in public wearing it, other young men try to throw him to the ground, so that he will dirty his *kafar*. Should they succeed, the shameful memory will follow him to his grave, but usually he manages to avoid the disgrace. A man must never be seen in public without a *kafar*.

More cultural clashes are occurring now between Yapese and visitors, as the tourist industry booms. The things outlandish tourists do! Some actually will *stand* on top of venerable pieces of stone money to have their pictures taken. Others whistle in public—doesn't everyone know that whistling is used only as a signal between lovers? Or visitors may go around patting a baby on the head (disrespectful), or offering to shake hands with an adult (undignified), or asking about a person's parents or other relatives (a gross impropriety, verging on profanity). "Will they never learn?" sigh the Yapese.

"Will they never learn?" sighed an American doctor as he patched the head of a teenager who had just done his second nose dive from a motor scooter in one day. But, the Yapese *are* learning—a new generation has discovered that fish comes easier from cans, that hot white bread tastes better than breadfruit, that candy, ice cream, soda pop, and sweet rolls are highly desirable. Teenagers love the speed of motorcycles and cars, and they display a new public freedom with the opposite sex, copied from Hollywood movies. Nor has the older generation remained untouched. Some—men and women both—wear Western clothes now when they go into town. Older Yapese can still build thatch-roofed houses and seaworthy canoes without making use of a single iron nail, but even they are beginning to find it more con-

venient to put up roofs of corrugated iron and zip across the lagoon in fiberglass boats with roaring motors.

Even on the atolls, modern technology is replacing old. Where once an outrigger canoe was necessary to communicate between villages, some chiefs now have walkie-talkies, allowing intervillage councils to be held by radio—until the batteries run down.

Atoll dwellers are a special kind of people, gentle, warmly affectionate, and easygoing, who speak in a soft voice seemingly pitched below the ocean's constant booming on the forever close reef. They dress differently than Yapese. Women wear wrap-around, loom-woven, bark fiber skirts and a flashing smile; men wear one-colored *thu*s and sometimes display elaborate clan tattoos, for the art is still practiced on these outer islands, having escaped the Japanese outlawing of it elsewhere. People of the atolls speak different languages, and even between residents of neighboring atolls the dialects sometimes make exact communication difficult.

Unlike a high island, with its rich and varied foliage, an atoll is little more than a fringe of waving coconut palms rising over the horizon. It is with the coconut, the atoll dwellers' staff of life, and their lagoon's larder of seafood that they must balance their precarious livelihood. Yet they are a strong people, possessing remarkable endurance and longevity.

Atoll dwellers know that one sweep of a typhoon and a high sea could leave their islets barren, with coral sands bleaching like dead bones under a tropic sun. And they know they must still depend on their ancient knowledge and skills, for they know they must live with the sea, not against it.

# Palau

Like emerald domes balanced on low pedestals, Palau's Rock Islands cast mirror images upon crystalline lagoon waters. Nowhere else in Oceania are there isles with this special scenic charm.

Except for half a dozen tiny isles beyond the long, broken oval of reef, the over two hundred islands of the Palau District lie on a north-south axis seven hundred miles from both New Guinea and Guam. Babelthuap at the northern end of the encircling lagoon is the largest island in the trust territory. It boasts ten villages and a population of over five thousand in its 150 square miles. Since the entire land area of the Palau District is only some 180 square miles, that leaves little solid ground to be divided among the rest of the islands. So here, too, are some of the tiniest trust territory islets—some hardly larger than oversized flowerpots. For twenty miles south from Babelthuap to Peleliu there stretches a wilderness of primeval islets whose stern cliffs are draped with tangles of vines, bushes, trees and flowers. The limestone islets have been undercut by eons of constant water wear so that now they rise columnlike from the lagoon.

Recently the Congress of Micronesia has asked for U.S. aid in preserving the Rock Islands as a trust territory park. Also being similarly considered are Truk Lagoon, as a war memorial, and the Nan Madol ruins of Ponape.

Palau undoubtedly played a vital role in the migrations of the Pacific peoples. Palauans are anciently related to both the Indonesians and Melanesians, so there is a wide diversity of facial type—although generally speaking Palauans share a light to medium brown skin color, black hair, and a medium build. Save for the most remote islets, they all speak the same language, a highly evolved and complex tongue that is difficult to learn.

Before foreign influence, Palauan society was highly organized and competitive. Each village usually had about ten clans of descending importance, the two highest being considered the aristocracy. A person's title, land, and social status were all determined by his or her mother's or mother's brother's position within the clan. Villagers were governed by titled chiefs of the upper two classes, who made laws in closed sessions, sometimes listening to a clan chief's requests, provided he was not too far down in the hierarchy. Villagers of the lowest classes kept their mouths shut and their hands busy, following the orders of the chiefs. Compulsory membership in clubs (with elaborately decorated clubhouses called *bais*) divided each village into competing sections that tried to best each other in such communal projects as road building, land clearing, planting, and fishing.

According to ancient Palauan belief, the origin of life on earth began when the god Tpereaki and the goddess Latmikaik rose together from a rock in the sea. The god chose the sky as his home, and the goddess resided at the bottom of the ocean. She brought forth many fish as well as two sons called "First in the Sky" and "First in the Lower World." The fish, through combined efforts, built a tower that rose above the water and became the first land—Palau. Then certain fish mated with the gods, and from this union came humanity.

Palauans' clan rank and food taboos depended on which fish and which gods were their ancestors. Each clan's gods and goddesses had personal names and held the same title as clan leaders. The gods of the village aristocrats' highest-titled clan became the village deities, honored with a centrally located shrine house, and before every community undertaking such as wars, celebrations, or intervillage relationships, offerings were made at the shrine. All villagers observed the food taboos of the village gods in addition to honoring taboos of their clans' ancestral spirits. The spirits of their more immediate ancestors, called *bladek*, were actively consulted via trance for help in solving personal problems or family affairs. The person bearing the title of clan leader was responsible as a "priest," and the left side of his or her residence was reserved as an altar where offerings were made when someone became ill or consultations were requested by family members.

The first foreign influence that was to change Palauan life came in 1783, when an English sea captain named Wilson and his crew were shipwrecked on an outer island reef. Treated as honored guests rather than (as they had feared) as tomorrow's lunch, captain and crew lived on the island of Koror during the three months that a new ship was being built for them, and, in return for the leading chief's hospitality, the Englishmen, with their firearms, helped the chief conquer the nearby islands. When time came to sail, the chief sent his son, Leboo, with Wilson, and the captain left guns, ammunition and an expert rifleman on Koror to teach gunmanship to the chief's men. Seven years later two British ships brought the news that Leboo had died of smallpox barely six months after leaving Palau. A portrait of Palau's first overseas scholar hangs in Koror's museum.

As a neglected part of Spain's Pacific empire, Palau had been visited by Jesuit priests as early as 1866, but harried by successful German traders, Spain's interest quickened. Between the years 1885 and 1889 the conversion of several chiefs made instant Catholics out of entire villages and ended intervillage warfare.

Having bought the islands from Spain, the Germans then imposed a planting quota of one hundred new coconut trees on every male islander. After Germany discovered phosphate deposits on Angaur, laborers were imported from Truk and Ponape. This introduction to other Micronesian cultures the Palauans found exciting and stimulating. Eager to learn, quick to adopt whatever new customs struck their fancy, they blended foreign elements into their lives—but deep beneath the surface many of the old ways still lingered.

Palauans recall the Japanese occupation with a sense of awe, and rightly so, for not only was Koror the governing capital for Japanese Micronesia, it also became the tropical vacationland for escapees from Japan's winters. A booming town that expanded to fifty thousand just before World War II, it had neat streets of government buildings, department stores, schools, shops, shrines, temples and Christian churches, theaters, cafes, geisha houses, and Japanese style residences. American bombers reduced it to rubble, and it has never completely recovered, although it is today the Palau District headquarters.

While the Japanese did not treat the islanders as equals, the Palauans, hoping to learn more about the strange but obviously successful ways of the outer world, hoped also to find new paths to greater wealth and power within their own society. It was Japanese industry that Palauans most admired, for they had always had a healthy admiration for financial acumen.

Long before arrival of Europeans and Japanese, the islanders had been, in their own way, "money mad," having developed two systems of currency—one for men and one for women (which they still use). Men's money, pieces of glassy pottery, porcelain, and colored glass, whose origins are lost in antiquity, was used for such purchases as canoes, dwellings, and brides. Women's money, tortoiseshell trays up to ten inches long, paid for feasts, foods, and services rendered in preparation of same. The total wealth possessed by a village or a clan was a well-kept secret known only to the eldest and highest-titled male member of the clan. Although each clan or village tried to amass as much money as it could, it always professed poverty.

Palauans are alarmed by the awakening interest that the United States Department of Defense is expressing in their district. After Washington began negotiations for return of Okinawa to the Japanese, visits by Pentagon officials became increasingly frequent. When one officer remarked that he found Palau much to his liking, the district legislature sent off a resolution to Saipan to the effect that a military base in the district "would not be in the best interests of the Palauan people," a statement as likely to be heard as a whisper against a typhoon—the Pentagon can weather any local storms of protest under the "strategic" umbrella of the U.N. mandate.

There is another side to the picture; it is not only the military who are interested in the trust territory. Since November, 1966, Peace Corps volunteers have been working throughout Micronesia. Howard is typical of the enthusiastic workers whom I met in Peleliu. A student of anthropology from a Wisconsin university, he was involved in agriculture in his duties on Peleliu. His idea for backyard gardens was accepted by the women of the village, and now Peleliu diets are supplemented with onions, radishes, Chinese cabbage, squash, and tomatoes —all new to islanders used to such tuber crops as taro, sweet potatoes, and cassava. He also is helping in the program to restore the nine-thousand-tree communal coconut plantation, which was partially destroyed by rhinoceros coconut beetles. The only postwar source of income for the islanders was the salvaging of scrap metal from the leftover implements of war, but now the supply is getting scarce, and many young people have already left the island trying to find employment elsewhere.

Renamed Kamital by the Palauan family he lives with, who has adopted him in the island tradition, Howard bears all the responsibilities of an eldest son. Knowledge of local language is a requirement of all Peace Corps workers, but Kamital is especially fluent, and his use of correct Palauan has encouraged young people to be proud of their mother tongue. In his role as a son, he spearfishes with his foster father to provide the main protein in a largely fish and rice diet.

His family's house, like most postwar Peleliu village homes, is made of unpainted scrap lumber and roofed with corrugated iron. The two-room interior is unfurnished except for a Japanese treadle sewing machine on an old fashioned Singer stand. Shelves along the walls hold woven pandanus leaf sleeping mats, a kerosene lamp, fish hooks, and other necessities. Meals are served from a small cooking annex.

Kamital's interest in the people of Micronesia has been intensified by his Peace Corps stint, and he plans to return to the United States for further studies in anthropology. He says, "I will definitely come back to Micronesia to work here as an anthropologist." For him, it will be like coming home.

# Truk

Today, in the heart of Micronesia, a fleet of warships waits—for a call to battle that will never come. Lashed to their decks are military trucks, crates of ammunition and stacks of gas masks. In the holds, sections of fighter planes await assembly, and wing guns lie silent. Mess tables, set with dishes, wait for a meal that will never be served. Anchor chains are down, and the ships will wait throughout eternity.

Once the pride of the Japanese fleet, the ships were sunk on February 17, 1944, in a surprise predawn attack by the dive bombers and torpedo planes from the United States Carrier Task Force 58.

Other evidence remains on islands in the Truk Lagoon,—cannons, generators, cranes, and sturdy concrete buildings—that identifies this area as the former headquarters of Japan's naval and air power in the mid Pacific.

Ideally suited to the purpose for which it was chosen by the Japanese, Truk Lagoon lies within an enormous circle of barrier reef, forty miles across at it widest point, with only four deepwater passes. Unlike other Micronesian atolls, the eleven main islands rise high in the center of the lagoon. The peak on Tol, the highest, is over fourteen hundred feet. A few million years ago, Truk was a single, mountainous volcanic island within its fringing reef.

The Truk District extends beyond the reef to include nearly a hundred atolls dotting a span of ocean three hundred miles wide and six hundred long. The district's total population of twenty-six thousand (the largest in Micronesia) inhabits only forty of the atolls and islands.

It undoubtedly played a strategic role in Pacific prehistory, and inevitably its inhabitants became some of Oceania's most proficient seamen. Like all Micronesian vessels, the Trukese sea canoe is of the single outrigger type, unlike the double-hulled Polynesian canoes. It may be as long as fifty feet, with a housing shelter built on a platform between hull and outrigger. The keel is usually carved from the trunk of a single breadfruit tree; sails, once made of woven pandanus fiber, are now canvas but are still of the lateen type, switched from a hinged mast to allow change of direction and to keep the outrigger always on the windward side of the vessel. Trukese skill in building great sea canoes is fast disappearing, but the spirit and seamanship that once carried a determined people across a trackless ocean wilderness are still very much in evidence.

For instance, five men from Pulap Atoll set sail one day for Truk, 150 miles to the east—an easy four or five days' canoe journey—to buy cigarettes. Thirty days later, the trust territory's interisland ship took them aboard, canoe and all, three hundred miles from their home. A storm had blown them off course to the west, and for a month they had lived on rainwater and raw fish. But they knew exactly where they were although they had no navigation aids—Ifalik Atoll in the Yap District, they claimed, was about thirty-five miles away. After computing by charts and compass, the captain of the ship had to agree.

With each Pacific island discovery, European explorers believed they were blazing new pathways across unknown seas, but the network of atolls between Micronesia's major islands had long been tradeways for sailing canoes. The outer islands of Truk District are atolls and lie within easy sailing distance of the high islands in Truk Lagoon. Everyone speaks basic Trukese, with different but understandable dialects, and for untold centuries the atoll dwellers have sailed to the high islands for foods not grown on their soil-poor atolls. They also sailed westward to Guam with trade goods—woven mats, coconut fiber rope, shells, and even their finely crafted canoes—while from Guam, with its early Spanish settlement, they carried back sophisticated implements of metal.

Truk had been sighted in 1528 by the Spaniard Alvara de Saavedra, who also discovered New Guinea's north coast and, hopefully, had named it *Isla del Oro*. No other Europeans came along for nearly three hundred years until a navigator named Dublon sailed into the lagoon and named it and a three-mile-long islet after himself. This islet later became Japan's naval headquarters. Dublon publicized his discovery so well that successive Russian and French expeditions explored the islands and marveled that these "primitive people" were knowledgeable about iron tools.

During the middle years of the nineteenth century, whalers stopped at Truk, but not often and not for long, preferring the more exciting ports of Hawaii, Tahiti, Ponape, and Kusaie. Then came the Germans, and major changes for the islanders. The Germans accelerated the palm-planting program, abolished warfare (which tended to slow copra production), set up trade stores and brought in their money, introduced Christianity, and wrote learned treatises on the strange ways of the Trukese.

With the flight of the Germans, many thousands of Japanese and other members of the coprosperity sphere—Koreans and Okinawans in particular—emigrated to the larger islands. They became owners of plantations, farms, fishing fleets, and shops.

Aside from the brief Allied attack on the Japanese bases, Truk endured no land battles. Probably the most devastating effect of the war came as a result of the American occupation of Guam and Saipan, which prevented the imperial navy from carrying supplies to Truk. The nearly fifty thousand people who had emigrated or who were stationed there were forced to live off the land—and the land was incapable of feeding them. It was a time of famine and of desperation and, rumor says, of cannibalism. After the war the United States Navy repatriated the remaining Oriental population to their homelands, and the Truk islanders began to adjust to their new masters.

The atoll people, being remote from activities on the high islands in the lagoon, continue to live much as always. Once again copra has become their main source of income, while on the high islands, in addition to their usual tropical fruits—mangoes, oranges, bananas, and introduced garden vegetables—the islanders now have a potential future income crop in cacao, a project initiated by the U.S. Fish still supply the main source of protein, whether they are caught by a cooperative fishing party of village women or purchased in the can at the nearest store.

Truk's future may lie in a growing tourist industry, now that there are regular jet services from Hawaii and newly completed hotels. Truk's beaches await sunseekers, and for underwater explorers, the imperial fleet waits—on the floor of the lagoon.

# Ponape

Just beyond where I stood, inside the high-walled court-yard of the Temple of the Ancient Rulers, ocean waves slammed against the reef as if in thundering anger at the coral barrier that protects the hundred or more semi-artificial islets that make up Nan Madol. The mysterious ruins nearly a millennium old were once twin cities and the heart of a dynasty. Now among brooding mangrove swamps and eager jungle brush, crumbling walls remain as a memorial to a past grandeur, a legacy for today's Ponapeans. How did they come to be there, those massive walls, shored-up islets, and temple enclosures built of huge, five-sided, basalt "logs," some over twenty feet long and two feet wide, weighing as much as five tons? They were carried from Ponape's volcanic cliffs, on the opposite side of the island; but how? How were they transported and how were they hoisted into position so as to erect walls forty feet high? Who had acquired the skill of using stone in "log-cabin" style, built so securely that they have withstood centuries of abuse by nature and man? Who were these early master builders of the mid Pacific? I asked the questions in the darkness of the cavernous tomb where once lay the bones of priests and kings. Only the sea answered, echoing through the chambers of the dead.

They came by sea, the story goes, two men, Olosohpa and Olosihpa, in a great sea canoe, seeking a place to erect a temple to their gods. They made five false starts, at various sites on Ponape, before finally selecting the offshore location. From the tidal swamps, they built up islets inside frameworks of basalt "logs." Nan Madol—"the Place of Spaces"—became the name as scores of artificial islets were raised along serpentine canals, navigable only at high tide.

After Olosihpa died, Olosohpa declared himself ruler of all Ponape, taking the title of *sau deleur*—"Lord of Deleur"—and founding a dynasty of Saudeleurs (no one knows how many, but legends speak of nine), who ruled from the islet called Pahnkedira (the "Forbidden Isle"). From there, from the high platform of a thatch-roofed house, they watched their people dining in the big feasting house and they listened daily to the melody of the *sakau* stones' rhythms as a shrub's roots were pounded into the thick, soothing Ponapean drink called *sakau* (known elsewhere in Oceania as kava). Outside the main gateway stood special stones where visitors left their spears, and just inside were other stones where offerings were laid.

Next to the sovereign's island stood high-walled Idehd. There, priests foretold the future by the manner in which sacred eels accepted offerings of specially pre-pared turtle meat. But the priests failed to foretell the future for the last Saudeleur, Sau Demwai—"One Who Fought"—who battled with the god of thunder, some say, over a woman. The angered thunder god fled to Kusaie, where he called on a clan member, Isokelekel, to avenge him. Isokelekel came to Nan Madol with his followers bearing gifts for the Saudeleur, who in return offered the visitors hospitality on a nearby islet.

At a prearranged signal, one of Isokelekel's warriors picked a quarrel with a warrior of Nan Madol—and the battle started. Hidden weapons suddenly appeared; Isokelekel led his men to victory; and the Saudeleur with his army fled to the main island. As they did so, one of the Saudeleur's men, in a parting shot, struck Isokelekel with a stone, blinding him. In admiration of the warrior's skill, Isokelekel made the man a general, and today his descendants hold a place of honor in ceremonial feasts beside the descendants of Isokelekel.

In former days, all the land had belonged to one ruler. Over four hundred years ago, after Isokelekel's death, his son, the Nanmwarki, gave the title of Naniken to his son, thus establishing dual titles for the rulers of Ponape. Their descendants traditionally intermarry, and since inheritance is through the mother, titles change with each generation.

Isokelekel had reapportioned the island, dividing it into five districts, which still stand today, instead of the previous three of the Saudeleurs, and each district, headed by a Nanmwarki and Naniken, is subdivided into smaller sections each headed by a chief, under whose authority related family groups live and work their clan lands. A Ponapean is born into one of more than twenty clans, his or her status being determined by the rank of his or her mother. Many Nanmwarkis ruled from Nan Madol before one became Christian, Nanmwarki Paul, and in 1872 he abandoned the "heathen" cities. (The present reigning Nanmwarki of Madolenihmw district lives on the shores of Ponape near Nan Madol; it is courteous for visitors to ask his permission before entering the ruins.)

Easternmost of the Carolines, the Ponape District consists of two high islands, Ponape and Kusaie, and eight atolls. Ponape, the second largest island in the trust territory, and Kusaie, the fourth, both have rich volcanic soil, with interior peaks rising as high as twenty-five hundred feet. These cloud-catching heights are responsible for heavy rains (averaging about two hundred inches a year) that help make the two islands among the most fertile and beautiful in the Pacific. Ponape, with its lush jungles, exotic flowers, crystal streams, many waterfalls, and the rearing black monolith of Sokehs Head marking the harbor of Kolonia, deserves to be called "Garden Island."

Two lonely atolls in the far south of the district are Polynesian in both language and culture, and Kusaie language and culture are related to those of the Marshalls, while Ponapean is spoken on the main island as well as on five of its neighboring atolls. So the district's population of nearly twenty thousand speaks three distinct languages.

During the middle nineteenth century, whalers found at Ponape and Kusaie a warmth of welcome that was distinctly lacking in such places as Truk, where the inhabitants were not averse to chopping up the crews to use as bait. Kusaie, in fact, grew so notorious for its hospitality that it soon attracted the attention of the whalers' natural enemies, the missionaries of New England. In 1850 arrived the black-clad Boston Mission, preaching damnation and salvation and the overwhelming importance of cloaking naked female flesh in shapeless Mother Hubbards.

The mission was as deeply opposed to the Pacific pirates who put into Ponape as it was to the whalers—and it convinced the Nanmwarkis of their error in tolerating pirates and whalers as well as pagan gods.

The islanders had even less resistance to foreign diseases than to alien religion. In 1854, a British ship put into Ponape to bury a victim of smallpox, resulting in a devastating epidemic that swept the island. Now, 120 years later, it has not yet regained its former population.

German copra traders had been established throughout the area for some time before the Pope's ruling aroused Spain's possessive instincts. Then a contingent of settlers, priests, and soldiers was sent to Ponape to set up an armed garrison at the present site of Kolonia. When the Spanish began deporting Protestant missionaries, a religious "war" broke out, which caused much confusion among the Ponapeans. Thirteen years later, when Germany became the new owner, the Protestants were welcomed back, and today Ponapeans may attend Catholic masses, Protestant services, and meetings of Jehovah's Witnesses, while they listen to admonitions of Seventh Day Adventists against certain "sinful" seafoods.

Under the old Ponapean land system, clans contributed "the first fruits of the harvest" to the hierarchy of land-lords. Unhappy at this diversion of copra profits, Germany instituted a land reform, issuing individual deeds to male clan members living on kin land; decreed that inheritance would be patrilineal instead of the traditional matrilineal; placated the rulers with "a guaranteed harvest, work quotas, and ceremonial feasts"; and retained for themselves (in fine print) the right to confiscate land for official use.

During the confusion over land reform, World War I broke out, the Germans left, and the Japanese took over, adding a few new rules but finding much to admire in the German confiscation clause. Colonization began; sugarcane plantations were established; rice and cassava were planted, processed, and shipped home to Japan; experimentation with many different tropical fruits and vegetables was begun. Then came another world war, and the abandoned sugarcane fields on the high interior plains were quickly reclaimed by hungry jungle.

Now the Agricultural Experimental Station near Kolonia, the district headquarters on Ponape, grows and distributes improved varieties of coconuts, sweet potatoes, papayas, bananas, and citrus fruits. The station has successfully established a growing industry in Ponape pepper and has overcome diseases that were attacking the cacao tree, which now promises to become an important source of future export. Unlike other Micronesians, Ponapeans are farmers rather than sailors or fishermen, living not in fishing villages but in homes scattered throughout the island. However, asking a Ponapean where his home is often leads to an evasive answer. After all the various land "reforms," he finds himself uncertain how to answer such a question.

# Marshall Islands

Like old scars across the ocean's face, the 1,156 atolls and reefs of the Marshall Islands pockmark some three hundred seventy-five thousand square miles of Pacific Ocean. The eastern edge of Micronesia, they lie about 2,000 miles southwest of Hawaii in two vertical lines, 800 miles long and about 130 miles apart. The eastern line is named Ratak, which means "Sunrise," and to the west is the line called Ralik, "Sunset." Only five could be called islands (flat coral uplifts as a separate entity within a fringing reef), but of the Marshalls' total land area of 74 square miles, these islands constitute only 1.72 square miles. All the other 1,151 "islands" are true atolls, coral reefs that scarcely show their teeth above the waves. The district's total population of nineteen thousand inhabits only twenty of the atolls and four of the islands.

The emotional attachment the Marshallese have for their home atolls is difficult for foreigners to understand. Each atoll's minuscule islets are scarcely more than drifts of coral sand caught along rims of reefs, yet they have a deep and spiritual meaning for the islanders born there. From the morning of their life to death they live within sight and sound of the ocean; always they see above them shaggy-headed coconut palms bending in constant trade winds; always they hear, forever throbbing, the beat of the sea pulsing against their land. Perhaps this precarious life at the edge of oblivion has rendered them the gentle people they are, who consider the most important personal virtue to be kindness. Even their softly spoken daily greeting, *yokweyok*—"love to you"—expresses this.

On the soil-poor atolls, constant care is needed to coax anything more than coconuts and pandanus to grow. The people know how to compost and use built-up vegetable beds. They know how to catch precious rain water—their only fresh water source. Yet the Marshalls are the leading copra producing islands in Micronesia. But monetary benefits from the coconut are recent—a foreign inducement. The atoll dwellers staff of life has always been the coconut tree, which grows well on atolls because of its ability to find fresh water that floats on top of heavier salt water beneath the coral sand.

A coconut palm lives for about a century and for about half that time it can produce as many as three hundred coconuts a year. From blossom to mature nut takes a year, and during development, the coconut has four edible stages. Inmature green nuts provide an always cool, thirst-quenching drink, a vital necessity on atolls where drinkable water is often nonexistent. At the second state, liquid is also present in addition to a soft jellylike and richly nutritious meat. From the meat of the mature nut, a thick cream is extracted, which is used as other people use milk. The last edible stage is the sprouting coconut, when the kernel becomes a sweet, spongy, cakelike mass.

Food, however, is only the first of many gifts granted by the bountiful tree. The blossom yields palm toddy, an intoxicating drink, forbidden by missionaries, but which recently has been discovered to be a prime source of vitamins and minerals. The nut's husk supplies fibers for rope and twine, necessary for building houses and canoes. Leaves are woven into screens, roofs, and baskets, and are also used as torches for night fishing. The silvery matting that forms around new leaves is used as ornaments, as a kind of wrapping "paper," and as fabric for garments. Out of the trunk come pillars and beams for houses, spars for boats, lumber for furniture, and wood for fuel. The dried ripe coconut meat (copra) supplies oil for the skin and hair, a healing salve for wounds, and a fuel for lamps. It is this final state that has captivated the Western world, for as copra, it is shipped off to worldwide commercial centers, where it is used in all manner of things, from soap to margarine.

For such a wonderous tree, all peoples of the Pacific islands have legends telling how this tree of life originated. From Ailinglapalap Atoll in the Marshalls comes the story of the woman, Limokare, whose second son was a green coconut. When he was born, he was a great novelty, for no one had ever seen a coconut before. In spite of his oddness, his mother loved him, admiring his little round eyes and mouth as she nursed him, which is why the coconut is full of milk. One day he told her to bury him alive. To console her in her sorrow at his unusual request, he described all the useful ways he would take care of her and her people. She acquiesced, tending the burial ground daily, marveling at how the first leaves looked like the wings of a flying fish. She gave a name to each stage of the tree's growth—names that the Marshallese know to this day.

Because the sperm whale bred in neighboring waters, the protected lagoons of the Marshalls were invaded, early in the nineteenth century, by rowdy whaling crews; then by pirates, by outlaws in stolen sandalwood ships, and by blackbirders. For over a hundred years these lagoons protected a horde of sea adventurers.

Into this lawless scene entered the authoritarian missionary. The first company arrived in 1852 and was soon followed by others. Their success in the Marshalls was even more remarkable than it had been in Hawaii, perhaps because the Christian concept of a god of love so nearly paralleled the Marshallese' own philosophy. Eager to please their new mentors who came armed with Bibles rather than guns, the islanders forsook their old gods for the new one, learned to be ashamed of their healthy nakedness, and donned all-enveloping clothes, even forcing their feet into shoes intended for New England winters. They replaced their traditional dancing and singing with hymns and prayers; copra money now went into the building of churches; and despite the fact that atoll land was at such as premium, Christian burial replaced putting a dead body into a canoe and sending it beyond the reef on its long westward journey.

Toward the end of the century came the copra-haunted Germans. Then, in 1914, the colonizing Japanese arrived, followed by the military, who built airfields on the islets of Kwajalein Atoll, the lagoon of which became the naval base from where aircraft carriers steamed forth one day toward Hawaii. In 1944 the United States dropped over fifteen thousand tons of explosives during a period of two months, in order to soften up tenacious Japanese defenses, before attempting to land. The U.S. military has never released its hold on the world's largest atoll (the lagoon is seventy-five miles long and fifteen miles wide). Under the strategic loophole, it has become a top-secret missile and antimissile base. Not even trust territory personnel are permitted there without permission.

Kwaj, as it is called by its four thousand American residents, offers them every convenience Americans have been taught to believe essential to happiness: beauty parlors, discount shops, supermarkets, country clubs, golf links, bowling alleys, swimming pools, tennis courts, and of course movies—four different ones are shown free every night.

An added attraction is that every family can have servants. Over four thousand Marshallese are crammed into neighboring Ebeye islet (once called "the slum of the Pacific") and are ferried daily to and from their jobs as laborers, maids, and gardeners. At one time Kwaj was due to be phased out, but recently it has become more active than ever, and more and more Marshallese are being moved from their own Kwajalein islets to Ebeye and neighboring Lib.

At least two other groups of Marshall islanders are unhappy about the strategic aspect of the trust territory mandate. These are the displaced people of Bikini and Eniwetok, whose atolls Washington declared, in 1946, would become sites for experimental nuclear explosions.

The 167 residents of Bikini were removed from their home lagoon, with its thirty-six islets, after only six weeks' notice. During the first two years of their exile, they were transferred three times until they finally ended up on the island of Kili, which is five hundred miles from Bikini—and wholly unsatisfactory. Having no lagoon, it is incapable of supporting its enforced residents; further, during several months of the year stormy seas often make it impossible for supply ships to land there. At the time of their expulsion, the Bikinians were paid $323,000 as compensation for "indefinite use" of their homeland, with the promise that it would be returned to them at some future date. Meanwhile, in the quarter-century of their exile, their population has almost doubled, so the annual income from the trust fund they set up with their compensation money is not even enough now to pay for the shipped-in food on inadequate Kili. Besides, they have a longing for home. Bikini is the spirit world of

their ancestors and of their children yet unborn. But that strong emotional tug that every Marshallese feels for his own atoll fails to arouse any similar emotion in the District of Columbia.

The people of Eniwetok are waiting too. In 1947, the United States Navy put 136 tearful Eniwetokese ashore on uninhabited Ujelang Atoll. What coconuts the island did produce were continually destroyed by an exploding population of rats. The exiles' pleas for help were finally answered. A government exterminator arrived, strewed poison about liberally, and killed sixty-five pigs. The DP's did not report the damage, disliking to cause trouble for the exterminator.

Although their place of exile is only 120 miles from their home atoll, the nearest inhabited atoll is 300 miles away, and the supply ship on which they depend is frequently late or—if the weather is bad—fails to appear at all. At one point, the situation grew so desperate that when the ship finally did arrive, the entire population went aboard and refused to leave unless the captain took them away. Having no authority to do so, he radioed for emergency supplies to be sent immediately, and he stayed until the supplies arrived.

Then the district administrator promised the exiles that adequate amounts of food would keep coming in the future, that the island's destructive rat population would be brought under control, that money would be supplied to repair dilapidated houses and decaying outrigger canoes, and—most important of all—that he would plead for their petition to go home. All the promises were kept, but the Department of the Interior refused to entertain the petition.

Still the Marshallese smile and greet strangers as they always have, with, *yokweyok*—"love to you."

Previous page: U.S. Sherman tank, sunk off Saipan's
Blue Beach Two on D-Day.
Below: Cross and helmet mark Saipan invasion site.
Opposite: Saipan sunset.

# Yap

Opposite left: United Nations Day
parade of school children, Colonia,
Yap.

Opposite right: Dancer, Yap.

Right: Dancers, United Nations Day
celebration, Colonia, Yap.

Below: Yapese boy with his *thu*.
Right: Mother and child, Yap.
Opposite: Footrace, United Nations Day celebration, Yap.

Left: Yapese high school students blend modern with ancient.
Below: High school students, Colonia, Yap.

Below: Yapese girl making a new grass skirt.
Right: Yapese girl on a village path.
Opposite: Boys on a homemade raft.

Opposite: Yapese lady with kitten.
Right: Makings for betel nut chewing: betel nut, leaf, coral lime.
Below left: Pounding betel nut, the method used by old men.
Below center: Applying lime to pounded nut and leaf.
Below right: Chewing the pounded nut with lime and leaf.

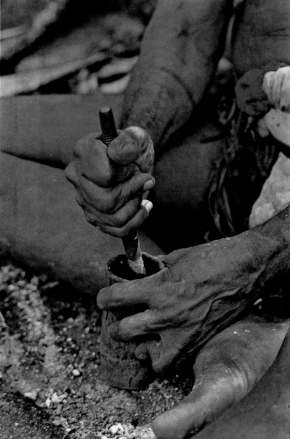

Below: Supermarket, Colonia, Yap.
Right: Yapese man with stone and shell money.
Opposite: Stone money on a beach; men's house in background, Yap.

# Yap District Atolls

Below: Outer Islands High School, Ulithi Atoll.
Right: Girls playing volleyball, Ulithi Atoll.
Opposite: Ulithi girls dancing.

137

Previous page: Mog Mog islet dancers, Ulithi Atoll.
Below: Ulithi Atoll chief.
Right: In the outer atolls, men of high rank once had
elaborate tattooing.
Opposite: Most Ulithi Atoll people are Christians.

Opposite above: An Ulithi girl weaves her own clothing.
Opposite below: Making sennit by rolling coconut husk fibers, Woleai Atoll.
Below: Lamotrek Atoll women.

Below: The trading ship *Yap Islander* at anchor off Elato Atoll.
Far right: Children playing, Lamotrek Atoll.

# Palau

Below: World War II Japanese aircraft sunk in lagoon, Palau.
Right: Lagoon and reefs, Koror area, Palau.

Above: Lagoon fish, Palau.
Right: Lobster, Rock Islands, Palau.
Opposite: Rock Islands area, Palau.

Above: Woodcarver, Palau.
Right: Men's house, Koror, Palau.
Opposite: Jeep painted with Palau legends, Koror.

Above: Palau legislature building, Koror.

Left: Koror school children admire Japanese motorcycles.

Opposite above: Palau legislature.

Opposite below left: Koror girl enjoying popsicles.

Opposite below right: Koror woman of high rank.

Above: Coconut palms.
Left: Entomologist Bob Owen studies the rhinoceros coconut beetle, destroyer of coconut palms.
Opposite: Islands in Truk Lagoon.

Truk

Below: Reef, Truk.
Right: Mast of sunken Japanese ship, Truk Lagoon.
Opposite above: Truk Lagoon.
Opposite below: Sunken Japanese ship, Truk Lagoon.

Below: Trukese boys, Dublon Island.
Right: Children playing in rain, Moen Island.

Women fishing in lagoon, Truk.

Above and right: Dancers from the Mortlock Islands, Truk.

Left: Children playing, Moen Island.
Opposite: Truk Lagoon at sunset.

Ponape

Left: Nan Madol ruins, Ponape.
Above: Basalt "logs" used in the construction of
Nan Madol.

Below: Children, Ponape.
Right: Rolling hoop in the rain, Kolonia, Ponape.

Opposite: Girls in a stream,
Metalanim area, Ponape.
Right: Waterfall, Metalanim area,
Ponape.

172

Opposite above: Pounding roots for making *sakau* (kava).

Opposite below: Pounding rock, roots, *sakau* drink.

Right: Plant pathologist Jim Zaiger experiments with cacao nuts at the agricultural experimental station, Kolonia, Ponape.

# Marshall Islands

Opposite: Remains of atom bomb test tower, Bikini Atoll.
Left: Atom bomb test bunker, Bikini Atoll.
Above: Displaced Bikini woman living on Kili Island.

175

Left: Majuro Atoll.
Above: Lagoon, Majuro Atoll.

Polynesia

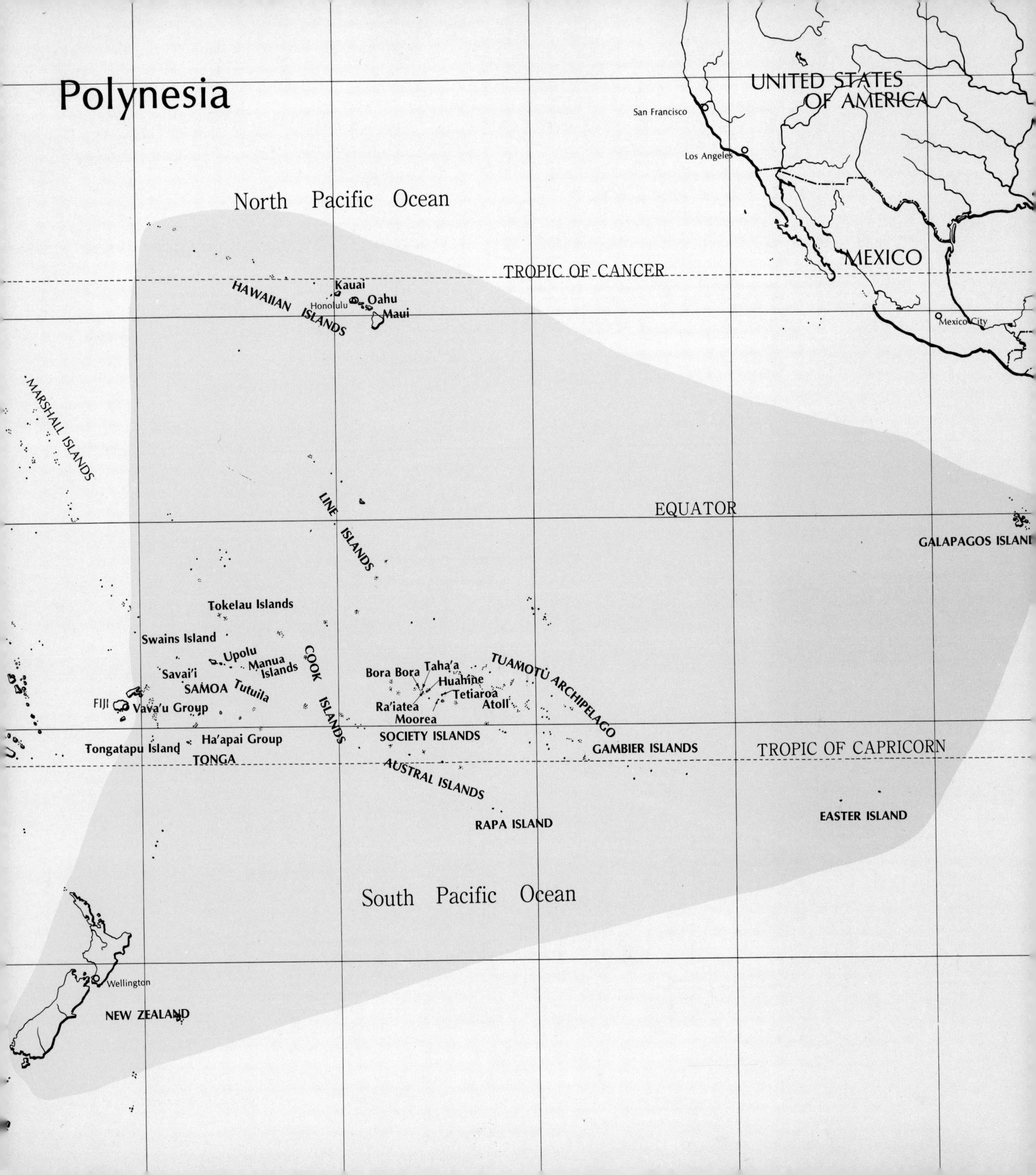

# Polynesia

North  Pacific  Ocean

UNITED STATES
OF AMERICA

San Francisco

Los Angeles

MEXICO

Mexico City

TROPIC OF CANCER

MARSHALL ISLANDS

HAWAIIAN ISLANDS

Kauai
Oahu
Honolulu
Maui

LINE  ISLANDS

EQUATOR

GALAPAGOS ISLAND

Tokelau Islands

Swains Island

Upolu

Manua
Islands

COOK ISLANDS

TUAMOTU ARCHIPELAGO

Bora Bora  Taha'a
Huahine
Tetiaroa
Atoll

Savai'i

SAMOA  Tutuila

FIJI

Vava'u Group

Ra'iatea
Moorea

SOCIETY ISLANDS

GAMBIER ISLANDS

TROPIC OF CAPRICORN

Tongatapu Island

Ha'apai Group

TONGA

AUSTRAL ISLANDS

RAPA ISLAND

EASTER ISLAND

South  Pacific  Ocean

Wellington

NEW ZEALAND

# Polynesia

This was the last great area of our planet to be occupied by mankind. The realm of Polynesia, with its hundreds of islands, flares across twelve million square miles of Pacific Ocean.

The Polynesian triangle stretches northeast from Samoa to Hawaii; from Hawaii southeast five thousand miles, past the Marquesas, to Easter Island, the east-pointing apex, which lies twenty-five hundred miles off the Chilean coast. Then the line turns south and west five thousand miles to New Zealand; and finally north again to Tonga. Within this huge Pacific pocket are numerous islands and atolls inhabited by a people known as Polynesians.

With few exceptions they are ruled by foreign governments. French Polynesia includes the island groups of Marquesas, Society, Leeward, Rapa, Austral, and Gambier, as well as numerous and often uncharted Tuamotu atolls and reefs. The fifteen Cook Islands, and the Tokelau Group of atolls have New Zealand as their guardian; Pitcairn, of *Bounty* fame, appeals to Fijian courts to settle disputes; the Galapagos Islands are under Ecuadorian rule; and the Line Islands, forgotten bits of land between Hawaii and French Polynesia are claimed by both Great Britian and the United States, which is also responsible for American Samoa.

Among these were the islands that caught the romantic fancy of Europe when their first South Pacific explorers returned home with glowing reports of beautiful high-mountained islands, rich with fruiting plants, inhabited by a gracious, golden-skinned people who had welcomed them with unlimited hospitality.

However widely scattered they may be, Polynesians are bound by a common heritage. They once honored the same gods, although different gods developed greater importance on distance-separated islands, and ways of worship varied. But universal in Polynesia were the twin concepts of *mana*, a supernatural power won or received by a person, or embodied in an object, and *tabu*, *tapu*, or *kapu*, a prohibition that could be placed on persons, objects, or areas, making them sacred or profane and therefore forbidden. Polynesian languages are similiar, although two islanders from opposite ends of the Polynesian triangle find communication difficult.

Throughout the islands, the birthland is remembered as Hawaiki, pronounced and spelled variously in various islands but always with the same meaning—a land to the west, the place of origin and the place a soul returns to after death. Exceptions are the earlier settlements of Samoa and Tonga. In one Hawaiki is the island of Savai'i, in the other, Ha'apai; but for both, their westward land of the dead is known as Pulotu.

When Europeans first began calling at Polynesian islands, the adventurers discovered a large-bodied, brown-eyed, hospitable people, with dark gold skin and Caucasoid features. Generally accepted now is the explanation that Polynesians came originally in at least two separate migrations from Asia by way of the Malay Peninsula, stopping at various Melanesian and Micronesian islands and finally settling at Tonga and then Samoa, Oceania's first purely Polynesian settlements. Carbon dating suggests that Tonga was occupied by 430 B.C., Samoa by 200 B.C. From here Polynesians initiated long, adventurous, eastward voyages to other islands in migrations that occupied many hundreds of years. Once again reference to carbon dating indicates that Polynesians were in the Marquesas by 122 B.C.; from there they ranged wide to Easter Island

about 400 A.D., to Hawaii around 750 A.D., and to the Tahiti group by 860 A.D. From Ra'iatea they migrated to New Zealand in 900 and to Hawaii again in 1300.

That these were deliberate voyages undertaken for the purpose of settling new islands, there is little doubt. Only on long sea expeditions were women allowed in the great sea canoes. Developed from the outrigger, the Polynesian open sea canoe was a double-hulled craft, sometimes over one hundred feet long. The ship was powered by paddlers and by wind-catching pandanus mat sails, while passengers were housed in a thatch hut on a platform laid between the twin hulls. To begin new generations of food animals, the migrants carried pigs, dogs, and fowl. Coconuts in various stages of ripeness furnished drink, food for animals and humans, and seed. Preserved breadfruit, yams, and freshly caught fish also provided food. The voyagers carried cuttings of tuber crops like taro, yams, and sweet potatoes. (The sweet potato, native to South America, is thought to have been picked up by Polynesians who journeyed to the continent and returned). Gourds held fresh water, and the great pandanus mat sails caught additional water from rains.

Masters of reading the ways of the waves and interpreting meaning from a bird in flight, the Polynesians knew well the solar sky, but they altered course by sighting stars through holes in a water-filled coconut.

By the time Columbus set sail with trembling crews, fearful of dropping over the edge of a world they believed was flat, the Polynesians had long settled every habitable island of the tropical eastern Pacific and explored no more.

# Tonga

Tonga—the unconquered. Of all Oceania's many peoples, only Tongans have never known the imposition of foreign rule.

This smallest kingdom in the world consists of about two hundred tiny islets stretching north 250 miles just above the Tropic of Capricorn. The northernmost island, a volcanic spit nicknamed Tin Can Island, is less than three hundred miles below Western Samoa, while Tongatapu, the capital island, at the southern end of the archipelago, is some two thousand miles northeast of Sydney.

Tongans had seen few tourists until 1967, when the "step into tomorrow" International Dateline Hotel (Tonga is just west of the jogged dateline) opened its fifty air-conditioned rooms in advance of the July coronation of His Majesty Taufa'ahau Tupou IV, perpetuator of the last ruling dynasty in Oceania.

Only the emperors of Japan and Ethiopia, among the ruling monarchs of the world, lay claim to a more ancient scepter. The royal line of Tonga traces its lineage back a thousand years into a blur of myth when the touch of Tangaloa, the sky god, brought into existence the islands of Tonga, Samoa, and Fiji. (However, Fijians credit a different god and have their own creation legend.) Having caused the islands to appear, Tangaloa sent a messenger, a dove, to plant vines on the new land;

and among the leaves, shapeless grubs were hatched. Tangaloa formed those grubs into the first men and women. Then Tangaloa descended from his celestial home to take a mortal wife, and of their union was born the first ruler of Tonga, the Tui Tonga. With other mortal women, Tangaloa conceived Tui Tonga's half-brothers, who became nobles and chiefs of the people.

As a descendant of the sky god, it was only right that His Majesty was the person to solve finally the legendary mystery of Tongatapu (and this he did, just two weeks before his coronation). The Ha'amonga-a-Maui is a huge trilithic arch with a morticed crosspiece, whose mysterious purpose had generated many theories. But at dawn of June 21, the shortest day of the year south of the equator, the king demonstrated that the first rays of the sun fell exactly on the carved lines on the crosspiece. Six months later, on the longest day of the year, examination supplied final proof that the Ha'amonga was used as a calendar to signal the time for planting, harvesting, and feasting in ancient Tonga.

In the meantime, on July 4, 1967, in the capital of Nuku'alofa ("Abode of Love"), Taufa'ahau Tupou IV, in a coronation ceremony complete with red velvet robes trimmed with ermine and all the precedential pomp and circumstance established by Britian's monarchy, His Majesty became king of Tonga in the eyes of the world. Two days later, at the Royal Kava Ceremony, he became ruler of his people in the mythbound Tongan traditional recognition of a new leader. The ceremony was held outdoors next to the white, Victorian palace, the king sitting cross-legged upon a tapa cloth and fine mat throne, while on the ground below him sat chiefs and nobles in a gigantic circle, each placed according to his rank and title as decided a thousand years ago. "The

Royal Kava Installation makes him really the king in the eyes of his people," Ve'ehala, Keeper of the Palace Records, told me.

As master of protocol for the occasion, Ve'ehala held the responsibility of ensuring that the kava ceremony, which lasted all day and into the night, proceeded without any infraction of the complex ritual governing seating and serving of more than two hundred chiefs and nobles; presentation of hundreds of gifts of fine mats, tapa cloths, pigs, and other foods; chanting of the admonitions by the three highest-ranking chiefs, telling the king of his duties and responsibilities to his people; and, finally, the calling out of each chief's correct kava-title as he received the cup.

The name Captain Cook bestowed upon Tonga—the Friendly Islands—is still used today, but what "Cookie" (as he is called in Tonga) failed to realize was that the islanders were not quite as friendly as he thought; in fact, it was only his own blithe assumption of their hospitality that prevented his being murdered in Tonga.

Eyeing Cook's ships with all their wonderful stores as well as that miraculous metal, iron, two chiefs argued one whole night whether or not to kill Cook and his crews and take the ships. By dawn, the chiefs had reached their decision—the prize was irresistible. Anticipating victory, they ordered a celebration feast. Then, unexpectedly, into the midst of the preparations came Captain Cook himself. As he stepped ashore, he assumed that the feast was to be held in his honor—and thanked the chiefs so graciously that they had no choice but to do as he expected.

Cook left two lasting mementoes of his visits. One was a tortoise, which died only a few years ago; the other was the tubercle bacillus, left there by his friend, William Anderson, who was traveling "for his health" as surgeon and a student of natural history—he died on the way home. It was on Cook's third voyage, in 1777, that he spent three months visiting various Tongan islands, after which he gave the Western world the first detailed description of the islands and their people. It was also in Tongan waters that mutineers, a few years later, relieved Captain William Bligh of his command of the *Bounty* and set him adrift in an open boat. Fortunately for Bligh, he had been sailing master of the *Resolution* during Cook's second voyage in the South Seas, so when he found himself in a small boat in those waters, he was not quite wholly at sea.

Those "friendly" islanders who so delighted Cook changed their policy shortly after Cook's last visit. Tongans traveling to Fiji to procure better canoes than they themselves could make took on some aggressive characteristics from the Fijians, who relished a rousing cannibalistic war and the resulting "long pig." Tongans came home bursting with newly acquired belligerence and a taste for human flesh. For years the Tongans waged wars against each other and even extended successful campaigns to eastern Fiji and Samoa.

Into this maelstrom, in 1797, sailed the London Missionary Society's ship *Duff*, which landed nine lay missionaries on Tongatapu. Of these, three were killed, while the others hid out in caves until rescue came. Twenty-five years later, a Wesleyan minister spent sixteen months on Tonga before admitting defeat. In 1828, two more Wesleyans arrived, and in 1831 the paramount chief was converted. Taking the name of George Tupou I, he was recognized as absolute monarch by other chiefs, after which he imposed Christianity, by royal decree, on all of Tonga.

Wars, famines, and imported diseases had ravaged the islands' population. Now a new era began under King George, aided by a Wesleyan minister named Shirley Baker. But other Wesleyan missionaries, making use of tithing as a competitive public demonstration were filling the coffers with islanders' money to send to church headquarters in Australia. Alarmed by this depletion, the king, supported by Baker, protested. In answer, the church excommunicated Baker; and the king promptly appointed him prime minister. Together they formed the Wesleyan Free Church of Tonga, while under Baker's influence the king renounced his exclusive ownership of all lands, surrendered the power of life and death that he exercised over his subjects, and instituted a constitutional form of government. Land was divided among nobles, according to rank, and among the people. The proclamation still stands today that gives, upon request, to every sixteen-year-old Tongan male, eight and one-fourth acres of country land, which he must actively plant and care for in order to retain ownership, and two-fifths of an acre of village land on which to build his house. No land is to be sold to foreigners.

When, at age ninety-seven, the king died, he was succeeded by his great-grandson, who took the title of George Tupou II. His quarter-century reign saw two highly important events for Tongans, and both occurred in the year 1900; on May 18, Tonga and Great Britian signed a Treaty of Friendship and Protection that lasted until 1970, when Tonga became totally independent. The other event had taken place two months earlier; on March 13, 1900, a daughter was born to the king and his first wife. She was named Salote (Charlotte) and was destined to become her country's best-known figure.

She ascended the throne at the age of eighteen, upon her father's death, having already married a Tongan noble, and for nearly half a century she ruled her islands lovingly but firmly and very conservatively, accepting the advice from a British consul. To the "outside" world, Queen Salote is probably best remembered as the majestic figure (she was over six feet tall) riding in an open carriage in the cold London rain during the coronation procession of Queen Elizabeth II.

While maintaining the constitutional guarantee of freedom of worship, Queen Salote succeeded in uniting the two antagonistic churches. Now Roman Catholics, Anglicans, Seventh Day Adventists, and Mormons have also built churches in Tonga and have established fifty-three denominational schools. There are seventy-six government schools, in which education is free and compulsory for all children between ages six and fourteen. Although high schools charge tuition, Tongans make every effort to give their children a chance at secondary education. Unfortunately, graduates trained for white-collar jobs have little opportunity for employment in Tonga, which retains its subsistence-agriculture economy. Its most important exports are bananas and copra; tourists may soon form a third major source of income.

Blue laws, written into the constitution, make it illegal to work or play, engage in business or go without a shirt on Sunday—but recently the laws have been stretched a bit. Taxis can now transport passengers to and from ships and planes, and the hotel operates, Sabbath or not.

The fast-growing population of Tonga is now nearly eighty thousand, of which some three-fifths are crowded onto the capital island of Tongatapu, (which means "Sacred Garden"). The island is less than a hundred square miles in area, with no running streams but with a fertile soil that makes it a continuous green carpet of banana groves, coconut plantations, taro fields, watermelon patches, and plots of garden produce. Still, there are too many people for the space and the food available —and the birthrate is doubling every twenty years!

Even so, the density of population on Tongatapu is not so high as on some of the other islands. The Ha'apai Group has a total land area of forty-five square miles— and a population of more than ten thousand. One of its islands has a density rating of 2,566 people per square mile. Of the thirty-four islets that make up the Vava'u Group, further north, only thirteen are inhabited. The largest, Vava'u, has a spectacularly beautiful deepwater harbor surrounded by high, once volcanic, green mountains. The island so enchanted a millionaire American yachtsman that he hurriedly sailed back to the capital in an effort to persuade the king to sell it to him. He failed.

It is really the people who make Tongatapu memorable, since the island itself is a flat-as-a-pancake coral uplift, hardly a traveler's idea of a South Sea island. But the people still greet the stranger with that warm-hearted Polynesian hospitality, which has yet to be cooled by too many visitors.

"You've come back!" cried my Tongan friend, Emma, the housekeeper at the Dateline Hotel. She held me tight to her ample bosom, and tears of joy flowed unheeded down her cheeks, just as—three years before—copious tears had marked the sadness of my departure. Then, as one of the three occupants of the just-opened hotel, Emma regularly had brought me home-baked taro leaves in coconut cream after she had learned of my fondness for the "good Tongan dish."

Another friend is Oscar Kami, who is the hero of a Tongan success story. Beginning as a ship's cabin boy, Oscar later served as valet to Britian's Prince Philip when he visited Tonga. When the hotel opened, he won the position of maître d'hôtel, at the same time continuing his duties as a minister. As his legal allotment Oscar selected land that no one else wanted—a bit of shoreline on the far side from Nukau'alofa, the island's only town. Rocky, full of debris-filled caves, the land was ostensibly undesirable, and far from any road, but Oscar had big plans for it. With the help of his family, working in scraps of time on days off, they built a road, cleared the jungle, cleaned the caves, swept the beaches, and planted gardens. He now has one of the most exotic settings for beach outings anywhere in the Pacific. Swimming in the protected lagoon is superb, the caves form natural amphitheaters, and Oscar can play host to as many as five hundred people for a day or evening of feasting and dancing Tongan style.

I remember with some embarrassment the generosity of a Tongan shell vendor. I had bought some seashells from his streetside display, and noticed the V-shaped scar on his forehead—a memento of a shark bite received while diving for deepwater shells. He told me about his four children, who he was putting through school, and invited me to visit him and his wife in their village the next day. When I told him (and truly so) that I was leaving the island the next afternoon for Samoa, he had said that he would bring me a small gift before my plane left. Early in the morning, he brought greetings from his wife and the "small" gift—a long length of beautifully painted tapa cloth, surely worth as much as the few shells I had bought. It was then that I committed a breach of Tongan etiquette—I offered to buy the cloth. "No, no," cried my friend, "It is our gift to you, so you will remember Tonga!"

# Samoa

The *taupou*, seated cross-legged behind the many-legged wooden kava bowl, leaned forward to knead and mix the powdered kava root with the water.

As guests in a Samoan village, my husband and I were being welcomed with an informal kava ceremony (women do not participate in formal kava). We were also seated cross-legged on several mats laid on the loose coral rocks of a guest house floor. Above us arched the dome of the building's thatch roof, braced with wooden beams lashed together with highly decorative bindings of coconut fiber sennit—not a single nail had been used in construction. Supporting the oval roof were many coconut palm pillars, each pillar now being used as a backrest for our hosts, the titled men of the village. Bare chested and wearing lavalavas, they sat Buddha-like at their proscribed posts according to their kava titles.

Already my legs were numb from assuming the traditional Samoan's sitting posture (to point feet at anyone is a Samoan insult), and I doubted that I would ever walk normally again, yet the courtesies had just begun! The *tulafale*, or talking chief, who was representing us had already thanked our hosts for a gift to us of the customary gnarled, dried kava root, and now the host orator was making a lengthy, eloquent Samoan welcoming speech, which would require a reply, also lengthy and eloquent, for Samoans do not believe in rushing protocol.

Meanwhile, the chief's daughter, the *taupou* (village hostess and ceremonial virgin), continued to swirl the kava, using a wadded bunch of hibiscus fibers. Suddenly she flung the strainer over her shoulder into the yard. A young man waiting there deftly caught it and made a dance of shaking it free of kava bark impurities before tossing it inside, where the *taupou* neatly caught it without looking back, and again worked over the bowl. She motioned for more water to be poured from nearby coconut shell containers, then tossed the strainer out again, and again. Our orator, with a careful eye on the girl, timed his finale with her signal that the kava was ready.

Another talking chief seated next to the bowl ceremonially addressed the group and announced that he was going to serve the kava. Everyone solemnly clapped hands several times, the orator then called out the kava-title of the highest-ranking chief, and the server presented him with the first cup. In proper order, according to his kava-title, each chief was served. Then the cupbearer approached me; holding his left hand respectfully behind him, he swept his right low, holding the half-coconut before me. "*Manuia*," I murmured, as I accepted the cup, tipping it to let a dollop fall onto the coral rock to salute the old gods, before downing the kava in one continuous swig.

Kava is a grayish colored, bland-tasting beverage with a slightly earthy flavor, but Samoans sometimes enliven it with a dash of chili pepper. Known variously as *ava*, *awa*, *kawa*, or *yagona* (depending on the island), kava was once used throughout Polynesia and still plays an important role in ceremonial as well as everyday life in Samoa, Tonga, and Fiji. Mixed a bit differently, it is also drunk in parts of Melanesia and Micronesia.

Missionaries usually banned it, and most foreign administrations outlawed it, while visitors to the islands, after their first drink, frequently compare the taste and sight of it to well-used dishwater. Only recently have outsiders taken a more favorable view of it. Scientific investigation has determined that the main ingredient of the root of a kava shrub (*Piper methysticum*) is a soothing tranquilizer. In large amounts it tends temporarily to paralyze sensory transmissions, which is why kava drinkers after a lengthy celebration feel that their legs have turned to rubber. However, lulled by the euphoria of overindulgence, the imbiber drifts into a deep sleep—and wakes with no hangover or other disagreeable after-effects. Nor is kava habituating. Oceanic peoples have long used it as a pain-killer, during tattooing, for instance, and as a medicine for ailing kidneys. It was also used as a cup of peace to seal a treaty of friendship, for belligerence disappears under the influence of kava.

The kava ceremony is only one aspect of *fa'a Samoa*, that oft-repeated phrase in the islands, which means "the Samoan way"—the way of our fathers. It has kept the Samoans strongly nationalistic, wary of changes that might threaten the traditional structure of their life, and made them capable of withstanding or absorbing the ways of foreign traders and missionaries. Today *fa'a Samoa* is facing its greatest challenge, as new generations brought up on foreign-taught theories of individualism and personal freedom threaten the old traditions.

In a traditional village, thatch-roofed huts stand in orderly rows around an open grassy area, the *malae*, where presentations, ceremonies, and dances are held. House walls are made of mats woven from pandanus leaves, which can be lowered to shield occupants against wind or rain—but they offer no real privacy. House foundations are of coral rocks, the height depending on the rank of the occupying family. A *matai*, leader of an extended family group called *aiga*, rates the highest foundation. *Aiga* (pronounced "ainga"—Samoan "g" is really "ng") is the Samoan "family plan," a kinship system that includes cousins thrice removed and in-laws. Bound by unwritten laws to assist, feed, house, clothe, give money to, or go to battle for their *aiga*, Samoans have little chance to build an individual, material empire—there is always some relative in need. Since marriages between *aiga* members are prohibited, the tentacles of relations reach beyond single villages and families and sometimes extend even to other islands.

Heading each complex family unit is "Big Daddy" or sometimes "Big Mama" (women may also become *matais*)—who is responsible for all members of the *aiga*. Chosen as leader by agreement within the *aiga*, a *matai* may be removed from both position and title if the relatives feel that family lands have been mismanaged, that poor judgment was shown in settling family quarrels, or if family funds are misused. He is held responsible for the welfare of all *aiga* members, while they in turn owe him obedience and respect as well as their labor and whatever money they earn. He mediates on their behalf in all matters outside the village, and his title requires that he be addressed in a separate language. In daily village life the size of his household varies, depending on how many relatives or children are "visiting."

A *matai* also holds the title of either *ali'i* (chief) or *tulafale* (talking chief); both positions include membership in the village *fono*, or governing group, which meets regularly to decide matters affecting village welfare. If his title is that of chief, he may not speak for himself in council but must depend on his orator to express, in the most eloquent terms, what he, the chief, has on his mind.

Ulcers, it has been reported, are a common complaint among Samoan patients at the Pago Pago hospital.

To visitors the Samoan way of life is merely confusingly intricate. But for foreign administrators eager to bring "a better way of life" to a people who believe they already have it, the pride of the people, their articulate manners, their elaborate courtesy, their concern for doing things properly—all part of the philosophy of *fa'a Samoa*—are especially frustrating. Politically there are two Samoas: the five eastern islands, with a total land area of seventy-six square miles, comprise the United States' only territory south of the equator. While Western Samoa, formerly a German possession and then mandated to New Zealand, has been an independent sovereign state since January 1, 1962. The two Samoas lie about twelve hundred miles northwest of Tahiti and some twenty-two hundred miles south of Hawaii.

Tutuila, twenty-five miles long, the main island of American Samoa, is the "typical" South Sea island of Western imagination. Rising in spectacular ridges from a narrow strand, it is almost bisected by the fjordlike harbor of Pago Pago. At one side of the harbor rears Rainmaker Mountain, fully deserving its name, as it makes Pago Pago the South Pacific's rainiest capital town. Sixty-five miles east of Tutuila are the three gemlike Manu'a Islands, volcanic mountains richly draped in heavy tropical growth and totaling four square miles when the tide is out. Swain's Island (actually an atoll), two hundred miles north of Tutuila, is a privately owned paradise of the Jennings family, descendants of an American who married the daughter of a Samoan chief.

Making up Western Samoa are two large islands, Upolu and Savai'i, and seven small attendant islands. All are mountainous and of volcanic origin. Savai'i, the largest Polynesian island outside of Hawaii, has peaks exceeding six thousand feet, while down the center of Upolu runs a spine of green mountains ranging from two to three thousand feet in height.

Legends tell of conquering Fijians and Tongans in the distant past, but their occupation seems to have had little effect upon *fa'a Samoa*, since the Samoans quickly gave up cannibalism, unlike Fijians, nor did they adopt the Tongans' divinely descended, hereditary chiefdoms, although they do share with Tongans a common creation myth. Like all Oceanic peoples, Samoans lacked a written language with which to record their history, but like all Polynesians, they developed into a fine art the recitations of genealogies and events. There is no doubt, then, that twenty generations ago the Malietoa family succeeded in driving Tongan forces from Samoa. The Malietoas were elevated, as a result, to the status of paramount chiefs, a distinction the family still holds today.

A Dutch navigator sighted the Samoan islands in 1721, but as he misjudged their location, no European found them again for forty years until Bougainville sailed through and, seeing a large number of canoes putting out from shore, hurriedly named the islands Navigator's Archipelago and continued on around the world. A few years later, La Pérouse stopped at Tutuila for fresh water (and other things as well, since he is blamed for introducing gonorrhea). During the course of his stop, a dozen of his men were killed and four times as many injured by the islanders as reprisal for the killing of a Samoan who had been caught stealing iron from the ship.

A British ship, searching for *Bounty* mutineers, stopped by in 1791, but the first real influence sailed into Samoa from the outside world forty years later aboard the *Messenger of Peace*, a home-built ship of John Williams of the London Missionary Society and his eight Tahitian teachers. Upon his departure, Williams left behind the Tahitian proselytizers—as well as the first influenza virus. Within six years, the island of Savai'i was deemed safe enough for six English L.M.S. missionary families to take up permanent residence. When Wesleyan missionaries also decided to undertake salvation of Samoan souls, the London offices of the two groups, after a certain amount of bickering, parceled up various islands, granting Tonga and Fiji to the Wesleyans and the Samoas to the London Missionary Society.

The islanders took to Christianity with the greatest enthusiasm. Welcoming the first missionaries as honored guests, the powerful chief Malietoa readily adopted the new religion and was soon recommending it to all his friends. *Matai*s all became deacons, and the missions' Samoan teachers were given a new rank, since Samoa did not have an organized priesthood of its own. Everyone went to church on Sunday, and villages began vying with each other to see which could build the finest and biggest church. Lack of funds left many unfinished. Christianity blended so smoothly into *fa'a Samoa* that one worried missionary wrote to his home office of the mission's failure because Samoans quickly took Christian practices into their own life-style. Nor were Victorian missionaries amused when they saw music-loving Samoans dancing the sensual *siva-siva* to hymn music altered to a Polynesian beat. Within forty years Samoans were not only completely Christianized, but were sending out Samoan "teachers" to Melanesian islands, most often with tragic results.

Following the missionaries' arrival came traders. In 1856, the German copra firm of Godeffroy settled in Apia and founded what was to become headquarters for their vast Pacific empire. When British and American trading companies also set up stations at Apia, Samoans suddenly found themselves in the midst of international commercial intrigue. To gain access to valuable coconut producing land, foreign companies favored different chiefs and began supplying arms to enlarge traditional intervillage arguments into full-scale wars. Soon the traders requested their governments to send warships to "protect" their interests, and by 1889 there were seven gunboats riding at anchor in Apia harbor, each waiting for someone else to make a move. With devastating swiftness, a typhoon roared down on the trapped ships. Germany lost ninety-two men and three vessels, while the United States lost three ships and fifty-four men; only the British gunboat successfully battled the storm and reached the safety of open sea.

Later that year, Germany, Britain, and the United States signed the Berlin Treaty, setting up an independent government in Samoa under "King" Malietoa, with the consuls of the three powers serving as advisors. The monarchy, however, was challenged by another Samoan chief—and the Samoans were at it again; and once again rival factions had the backing of foreign powers. In 1899, the Berlin Treaty was annulled; Germany annexed Western Samoa, the United States Navy took over the eastern islands, with Tutuila as a coaling station, and England went home.

With the First World War, New Zealand assumed control of German Samoa and, after the war, was granted a League of Nations mandate over the islands. Western Samoans, bitterly resenting the assumption that they were incapable of governing themselves, formed a resistance movement called *Mau*, and took as their battle cry "Samoa for Samoans." New Zealand administrators, who were mostly military men, replied with a call for warships and a show of force. Dissidents were exiled, and *Mau* supporters fled into the mountains. The conflict continued for sixteen years, until a change of government in New Zealand resulted in a change of administration policy in the islands. Samoans were given a voice in the management of their own affairs but they were not granted the independence they so ardently desired.

When the Second World War broke out, the Allied powers suddenly remembered those forgotten islands of Samoa, and there came a deluge of personnel and equipment, which invigorated the flagging Samoan economy. After the war, little was altered in administration of the islands save a change in wording. Western Samoa, from being a League of Nations mandated territory, became a trusteeship territory of the United Nations, remaining under the supervision of New Zealand. By this time Samoans had become upset about never being consulted on the destiny of their islands. A committee of Samoan leaders drafted a constitution, and, in 1961, all adult Samoans were asked to vote on whether they approved the constitution, and whether they wanted independence in 1962. They achieved their goal—and, for the first time in Samoan history a major decision was reached by consensus rather than by a *matai* speaking for his *aiga*.

American Samoa, which was under navy rule for half a century, did not have the same problems as Western Samoa, because naval administration did not intervene with Samoan politics unless it interferred with the navy way of life. However, the navy did make it mandatory for each village to build toilets on stilts at the edge of the lagoon—on the unworkable premise that the tides would act as nature's sewage system. These desecrations of the beautiful Pago Pago bay lasted well into the 1950s.

Education of elementary school children was a failure too, and finally education was left to the missionaries. The navy did organize a successful nurse training program and a police force with lots of spit and polish.

Then, in 1951, administration of the islands was turned over to the Department of the Interior under a politically appointed governor. There is a bicameral legislature, with *matai*s serving as senators and with representatives elected by universal suffrage.

The usual imported diseases have taken an unknown toll of Samoan lives. A naval census in 1900 showed only 5,060 islanders. By 1951, when administration was changed to civilian authority, the number had increased to over nineteen thousand, and it is now well beyond thirty thousand. The Samoan birthrate is approximately ninety new Samoans arriving every month, compared to a monthly death rate of four persons. So many Samoans have emigrated to Hawaii and the continental United States (the islanders are American nationals) that it is believed there are more Samoans abroad than at home. Until recently education was at minimal levels, so most Samoans going abroad could qualify for only low-paying unskilled jobs. A unique program of educational television, however, has raised the standards within the past few years to compare favorably with the United States.

One of the results of this increased education and travel is a generation with newly acquired desires to enjoy the American standard of living, which cannot be fulfilled under the old subsistence way of life. Many young Samoans, therefore, are rejecting the *matai* system in favor of personal independence; they no longer want to share all their possessions and wages with the *aiga*. *Fa'a Samoa* may soon become "the good old days"—a memory of the way it once was in Samoa.

# Tahiti

No sky, no sun, no moon, no stars, no land, no seas, no humans, no living things existed. This was Po—the formless, primordial void in which revolved Rumia, the egg-shaped shell. Within that shell, yet within still another shell—therein dwelt Ta'aroa, the Creator—alone.

Five Po eternities passed before Ta'aroa came forth to cry into the void. When no sound returned, he slept again in his shell within the shell as eternity followed eternity. Then he moved again, he overturned the outer shell to make a dome, and the inner shell he molded into a rock base to become Te Tumu, the Source—and so the world began.

Then Ta'aroa created Tu, the god of stability, and together they secured the sky-dome with pillars, naming the space beneath Atea, the sky goddess; the abyss of the underworld they called Rua. Ta'aroa now evoked more gods—Ro'o, god of fertility and of fruiting trees and plants; Tawhiri, god of storms and of the four winds; Tangaroa, god of fishes and the sea; Ra'a, god of stars; and Tane, god of forests, birds, and beauty—and on these gods Ta'aroa bestowed great *mana*. Then he created lesser gods and goddesses and demigods, and together all the gods furnished earth and seas and skies.

Now Ta'aroa instructed Tane to create Tiki, the first man, as a mate for Hina, who was a goddess and the first woman. From their children, who took as mates other gods and goddesses, descended the chiefly families of what we now call the Society Islands. The common people were conjured up by Tiki and Hina to help them in the earth world. As emblems of their divine heritage, the chiefs wore sashes of sacred red feathers, symbolizing the umbilical tie between gods and men. A permanent part of this girdle was a needle of human bone, which was used to add a few more red feathers at the beginning of each new reign. One chiefly family in Ra'iatea treasured a sacred sash that was twenty-one feet long and six inches wide.

It was on Ra'iatea long ago, which in those days was known as Havai'i, named for the place of origin, that gods descended from ten heavens for a ceremony in a *marae*, an open-air temple. It was essential, during this holy time, that absolute silence be observed, for when gods came to earth they came as birds and rested on specially built perches in the *marae*. Noise might anger them or frighten them away, so everyone stayed within his hut, dogs were muzzled, and roosters were hidden in dark cages to prevent their crowing; even the winds were still lest they rattle the palm fronds.

But one foolish girl went swimming in the river, and because of this impious act, a part of the sacred Havai'i turned into a giant fish frantically struggling to free itself. When it broke away, some of it fell and became the island of Taha'a; when the great fish had swum beyond the lagoon, another piece became Bora Bora and still another, Huahine. Finally the god Tu came and directed the fish toward the east, where at last it stopped. Its high dorsal fin became Oro-hena, Tahiti's highest mountain, and a second fin became the island of Moorea. To make sure that the fish would never swim again, the island's hero, (some say it was the demigod Maui) cut the sinews of the fish's throat; and its head, falling back, made Tahiti-iti (little Tahiti),which is joined by a narrow isthmus to Tahiti-nui (great Tahiti)—and thus Tahiti Island was formed and thus it remains to this day.

Tahiti was my first tropical island, and the memory of my first sight of it grows mellower with passing time. There was no airport then, when I first went there a dozen years ago. Our ship made landfall just as dawn slit the eastern horizon. After long days at sea, that dark scar of land seemed unreal, mysterious, full of exotic promises. Clouds tinted apricot and rose clung to the peaks of high, green mountains, shadowed valleys were veiled with a lavender haze, golden sunlight ran fingers along the edges of crests and ridges as the sun rose higher. We approached the white froth line made as waves pounded fortissimo upon the keyboard of the reef, then the sea roared a farewell crescendo as the ship rushed through a break in the knife-edged coral, and we glided into a lagoon colored a thousand tints of green and blue.

So it must have appeared to the Polynesians, in their hundred-foot double canoes, when they first glimpsed Tahiti, a couple centuries before adventurous Vikings sailed toward North America. So it must have seemed to Captain Samuel Wallis when, in 1767, he "discovered" Tahiti, claimed it for Britain, and named it after King George III. So too, a year later, it appeared to the French navigator, Bougainville, who claimed it for France and called it La Nouvelle Cytheré.

And so it must have seemed, yet another year later, to the commander of the *Endeavour*, James Cook, who was sent to Tahiti by the British Royal Society to observe the passage of the planet Venus across the sun. Although his observation was of little lasting scientific value, his observations of the Tahitians caught the imagination of the Western world. Cook visited Tahiti on all three of his Pacific exploration journeys, and he left his name to a beautiful bay on nearby Moorea. He explored Ra'iatea, Bora Bora, Huahine, and Rurutu (which is now considered in the Australs); and he gave the group the name Society Islands because of their proximity and the cultural similarity of their peoples.

All are volcanic high islands, though the stormy volcanos have long since died, leaving ruggedly abrupt mountains that are totally covered with vegetation.

The islands' lands are still divided among descendants of chiefs whose *mana* in the old days was considered so powerful that they were carried on the shoulders of slaves when they ventured from their houses, for if a chief touched the ground, it became *tabu* and forbidden for use by his people. Being of divine origin, chiefs also constituted the priestly nobility—all chiefs could trace their genealogies back to godly ancestors. Adherence to restrictions and taboos set by chiefs and gods bound Tahitians to a far more rigid and regulated way of life than the Christian way that was to come later and to topple the old gods.

Polynesian standards of beauty gave highest priority to whiteness of skin and corpulence. There were special fattening and bleaching houses for members of the nobility and for children, who, after weeks of isolation and overeating, competed in "beauty contests." Chiefs and chiefesses were always huge. Another mark of beauty was tattooing. In Tahiti, legs, thighs, and buttocks were decorated; but in some other Polynesian islands the entire body became a tapestry of painfully acquired tattoos. The first Western sailors to be tattooed were thus decorated in Tahiti.

Women's hair was cut short and was dressed daily

with fresh flowers; men plucked their beards and body hair with tweezers made of clam shells. Baths were taken several times a day, and bodies anointed with flower-scented coconut oil; body massage had been developed to a fine art. The people wore togalike clothing made of tapa, the pounded bark of the paper mulberry tree. Sexual experimentation was encouraged among the young, and at puberty personal instruction in the arts of love was given to both girls and boys by experienced older men and women. Marriage, with its maze of restrictions, usually was arranged by parents, whose duty it was to ensure that class and clan lines were not violated. For nobles, it became vital not to marry into a family with lesser *mana* than their own. Unsatisfactory marriages could be dissolved.

Within the marriage, on the other hand, certain privileges were granted that shocked puritanical Europeans and gained for Tahiti the reputation of moral laxness. A guest in a Tahitian home was honored by the wife's offering herself as a bed companion; refusal would be considered insulting to Polynesian hospitality. Husbands could chose to have sexual relations with their wives' sisters; wives, with their husbands' brothers. On journeys away from home, the husband customarily accepted the female hospitality of other Polynesian households, while the wife did not pine alone but took as her companion, for the duration of the separation, her husband's brother or some other partner.

When white men began calling at their island, Tahitians offered them the same sexual hospitality that they had always extended to their fellow Polynesians. This arrangement met with hearty acceptance by the first callers—explorers, whalers, and other adventurers—but missionaries were shocked and horrified when a Poly-

nesian wife offered herself for the night. Their rejection of the women was naturally considered an insult.

Overpopulation was a problem before the coming of Europeans. Even with constant wars and migrations to other islands, the birthrate always surpassed the death rate in these islands of gentle climate, plentiful food, and few diseases. So *arioi* society members, influencial in the islanders' lives, vowed on initiation to destroy all children born to them during their membership term. Under the tutelage of the god Oro, the *arioi* might be compared to a traveling revival meeting. Oro (known also as Ro'o) was originally a fertility god (although later he became known as Oro-of-the-laid-down-spear, a god of peace). Tamatoa, a chief on Ra'iatea who traced his lineage back to Oro, was leader of the first *arioi* society, branches of which soon spread throughout the Society Islands.

Anybody might join the society after meeting rigorous qualifications. Members devoted all their time to dancing and singing, to poetry and plays, and of course to worship of the tutelary deity. Since the latter was a fertility god, dances and dramas in which sex played a major role were part of the repertoire. It was performances of the *arioi* that astonished the first visitors, including Captain Cook, stimulated and delighted crews of whaling ships, and left missionaries without adequate words by which to describe the scandalous goings-on to church headquarters in London.

Tahiti's trials with Europe's men of God began in 1797, when the *Duff* arrived bearing emissaries from the London Missionary Society—four ordained ministers and a group of enthusiastic and devout laymen with knowledge of "practical" skills. For some of these, the Tahitian escapist dream became reality—they succumbed to the lure of the island's lovely women and fled beyond the wrath of their sterner brethren. The others persevered for a time, but after experiencing several years of scornful tolerance, only seven members of the original company remained on the island, still trying to convert Tu, a secondary chief whom the missionaries considered the "king" of Tahiti. After losing a war to more powerful rivals, Tu was exiled to Moorea, along with a stubborn gentleman named Nott, who was a bricklayer by profession, while the remainder of the mission fled to Australia. The defeated Tu, annoyed with his Polynesian god, finally submitted to Mr. Nott's persuasion and was baptized. He then, deliberately and publicly, broke a taboo —he ate a turtle without first performing the required ritual. When, to the general astonishment, he did not drop dead on the spot, some seven hundred of his followers decided that they, too, would embrace the new religion. Backed now by a host of newly returned missionaries as well as by his newly converted army, Tu ascended the "throne" of Tahiti as Pomare II. His *mana* rose to heady new heights.

So did that of the British missionaries, while the number of taboos they imposed increased geometrically. Dancing and singing (except hymns, of course) were outlawed; even the wearing of flowers was forbidden. The *arioi* society was banned, and its festive interisland canoes rotted on the beaches; so also did the great canoes of war. Required to wear European clothes, Tahitians no longer made their traditional tapa cloth; since kava was forbidden, that, too, was no longer grown or prepared. Ships' crews were not allowed ashore after sundown; mission spies peered behind bushes and peeked into houses in an attempt to catch "illicit" love makers; mission soldiers, armed with clubs, made sure that everyone, properly clothed, went to church on Sunday.

The Bible was translated into Tahitian (with the help of Pomare II), and the old temples and the images of the old gods were destroyed in an orgy of Christian zealotry. (A few images, kept as curios by missionaries, eventually made their way into European museums.)

Meanwhile, money was needed to continue spreading the "good word" among the islanders, and the money had to come from the islanders themselves. Copra was to pay for the new religion. Instead of waging wars, chiefs were now competing to fulfill quotas of dried coconut meat for the Lord, and commoners bore the burden of filling the holds of the mission ships sailing to Australia. Traders fared well, too, for of course converts required decent Christian clothing, and the houses of the missionaries had to be suitably furnished.

The reaction came not long after the death of Pomare II, when his young daughter assumed reign as Queen Pomare IV. In 1827, a Tahitian deacon of the mission church declared himself to be the new messiah, inviting islanders to follow his teachings, which had overtones of the old *arioi* society, including dancing, singing, and sexual freedom, and of the Bible-reading and praying of the new religion. After the queen herself joined the *Mamaia* cult, which had quickly swept the whole island, missionaries sent its leaders into exile on Ra'iatea—where it soon won new popularity and swiftly spread to the neighboring islands of Taha'a and Bora Bora. It was three years before the missionaries, led by George Pritchard of the Papeete mission (who later became British consul), regained control of the situation.

In 1836, two French Catholic priests sought to establish their religion on Tahiti and were bodily carried off the island, under Pritchard's orders and the queen's command, and put aboard a departing ship—an act that precipitated complex political events, resulting in several years of bitter French-Tahitian relations as well as putting a severe strain on relations between France and England. Eventually the queen accepted a French protectorate, while the British government made no attempt to interfere with growing French influence in Eastern Polynesia. Papeete is now the capital of all of Polynésie Francaise.

In the 1860s, because of the Civil War in the United States, cotton was in high demand, and an Irishman named William Stewart decided that Tahiti would be a good place to grow it—and so make his fortune. After considerable difficulty, for Tahitians did not want to sell their land, Stewart succeeded in obtaining several thousand acres, only to be met by the refusal of Tahitians to work the cotton fields. Undaunted, he arranged for the importation of a thousand Chinese laborers, and soon cotton of fine quality was being exported from Tahiti to Europe. Some years later, however, cotton prices fell, and so did Stewart's empire; thirteen years after he founded it, he died penniless, and the only remnants of Tahiti's cotton-growing era are its Chinese inhabitants.

Through immigration (which was not halted until 1930) and natural increases, Tahiti's Chinese today number over ten thousand. They are in all professions and businesses; they are merchants, tailors, planters, shipowners—half of the yearly business licenses are issued to Chinese. Even if they have been born in Tahiti, they must undergo a number of formalities to become French citizens, and few of them do; most hold Republic of China passports. They have their own clubs and tend to keep to themselves socially. Not many intermarry with Tahitians, although there are many mixed children. Illegitimacy is no stigma in Polynesia, where all children

are loved, and some of the islands most beautiful women are Tahitian-Chinese.

With the islands' Chinese taking care of business, with the French looking after government, and with religion now a free choice, the Tahitians were able to relax and go back to the good life, dancing and singing, fishing and gardening. In recent years, the population has increased steadily and today it is greater than when Cook first saw the islands, although few Tahitians will make claims of pure Polynesian ancestry.

A few years ago the French began using some of the Tuamotu atolls for nuclear experiments, and, although they lie eight hundred miles away, many of the necessary personnel are quartered in Papeete. The result is a foreign population boom. A city of twenty thousand, Papeete is bursting at the seams with new buildings and luxurious residences.

It is also the capital of one of the most expensive islands in the Pacific. There are deluxe air-conditioned hotels of two and three hundred rooms. There are golf courses and swimming pools; there is French cuisine; and there is deepsea fishing—for the energetic visitors, while black sand beaches edging sparkling lagoons lure even lazy tourists to vacation in Tahiti. Night and day the jets roar into Faaa International Airport, and small airports on Ra'iatea, Moorea, Huahine, Bora Bora, and the Tuamotu atolls put these islands within easy reach of the package-tour traveler.

Not long ago, at the Bali Hai Hotel in Moorea, I asked an elderly couple from Nebraska if they had enjoyed their stay in Tahiti. "Oh my, yes!" the wife exclaimed. "And, you know," she added, "we feel so lucky to have been able to see it before it changed."

# Hawaii

Time, in ancient Hawaii, was measured by the moon's cycle, and the twelve yearly moons were apportioned among the greatest Polynesian gods—Kanoloa, Kane, Ku, and Lono—the gods who had journeyed with emigrants from the Society Islands where they were known as Ta'aroa, Tane, Tu, and Ro'o.

Thus it was that the period from what is now October through January was sacred to Lono, god of fertility and cultivated plants and peace. During this time, called Makahiki, fishing and wars and work were forbidden while Hawaiians paid homage to Lono with gifts of pigs and harvested fruits and vegetables. This also was the time when harvest payments were made to the chiefs, the *alii nui*, who owned all the land. But once the paying of debts was over, there came a time for sports and games and for feasting and dancing, while the priests chanted prayers at the special temples, the *heiaus* of Lono.

Lono came to earth, legend says, on a rainbow bridge and, having taken Kaikilani, a mortal, to wife, lived happily for a time at Kealakekua Bay, which means "Pathway of the Gods," on the island of Hawaii (named for the Polynesian land of origin). But Lono was a jealous god and one day, convinced that his wife had been unfaithful, killed her in a fit of anger. Then, driven mad with sorrow at his folly, he traveled about the island, challenging all warriors to wrestling matches, after which he built a great sea canoe and sailed from Kealakekua Bay, promising that one day he would return on a floating island with many wonderful gifts. Centuries passed, but Lono did not return. Still the people waited.

On January 18, 1778, the waiting ended for the people of Kauai Island, with the appearance of two ships with wonderous white sails. The islanders had watched the strange looking vessels sailing around their island, and when they finally dropped anchor in Waimea Bay, the high chiefess of Kauai called a council of the *alii nui*. She argued down the suggestion by other chiefs that they kill the crews and take the ships for their metal (Hawaiians knew about iron from ships' debris that had washed ashore). This could only be Lono, the chiefess had told them, for were not the sails of the ships much like the great tapa cloth pennant carried every year in the name of Lono? Was this not the season of Makahiki when Lono had promised to return? The people must therefore honor the returned god and pay him proper tribute lest he grow angry and cause next season's crops to fail. She herself, said the chiefess, would send her daughter to be a companion for Lono.

Early on the morning of January 20, Captain Cook sent three armed boats ashore to find fresh water for the *Resolution* and the *Discovery*. The islanders crowded close about the landing party—too close for the peace of mind of one officer, who shot and killed a man. Later, that afternoon, when Cook himself stepped ashore, the large crowd of waiting islanders fell fearfully to the ground. Making use of sign language, Cook bade them rise. At this, a priest approached, chanting prayers; then offerings of pigs and bananas were laid at Cook's feet. He promptly made return gifts of cloth, knives, and nails. Friendly relations now established, the two crews were welcomed ashore. They, too, left a "gift" for the hospitable is- landers—syphilis.

Cook also visited Niihau for four days before continu- ing on his mission to find the rumored Northwest Passage. Nine months later, unsuccessful and driven south by the coming winter, he came back to the islands where he had been received so lavishly. The ships made first landfall at Molokai. There canoeloads of islanders offered a welcome, for by then word had spread throughout the islands of the previous visit to Kauai and Niihau during the last Makahiki, and now it was Makahiki again and Lono had returned as legend had promised.

For over six weeks Cook's two ships sailed around the island of Hawaii. Then completing his circuit, he selected Kealakekua Bay—the "Pathway of the Gods"—as his final anchorage. For the Hawaiians who had followed his ships' offshore tour, his choice of the legendary home of Lono was proof enough that this was truly the returned god, and thousands of welcoming canoes hurried out to surround the ships. Cook noted favorably that no one carried weapons. Of course, he did not know the story of Lono nor was he aware that these were months of peace when war was taboo.

January 26, 1779. The paramount chief, Kalaniopuu, who had been absent, returned and, heading a stately parade of double canoes, with priests and feather-dressed idols, he invited Cook ashore. Once there, the high chief took off his great gold and red feather cape and draped it about Cook's shoulders. He placed his crested helmet upon Cook's head, and at his feet the chief laid more feather cloaks and offerings of food.

For seventeen days everyone feasted and celebrated; then, during the last days of January, Kalaniopuu made signs indicating that Cook should leave. Neither Cook nor anyone in his party had understood why they had been received so royally, nor did they now know that Makahiki was ending and that the next months were dedicated to Ku, the god of war. It was time for Lono to depart; and indeed, on February 4, 1779, he did just as legend predicted—after a last gift of provisions from the islanders, he lifted anchor and sailed away.

Four days later, when a gale damaged the *Resolution's* mast, Cook decided to return to Kealakekua Bay to repair it. Anchoring at their old spot, the men were surprised when no canoes put out to greet them. Sending a party ashore, Cook learned that Kalaniopuu was absent and that a taboo was in effect. Nonetheless, the mast was taken off and repair began. When the para- mount chief returned, he visited Cook; his attitude at seeing the captain again was coolly courteous.

February 13. While filling some water casks, islanders helping men from the *Discovery* were ordered away by some chiefs. A scuffle ensued, and Cook's men damaged a canoe belonging to Chief Palea, and the chief was knocked down with a paddle. Nevertheless, he prevented the islanders from stoning the white men. That night to avenge their chief, some of his people stole a small boat from the *Discovery* and broke it up for metal.

February 14, 1779. Cook, angered by the theft, ordered his marines to patrol the bay entrance in small boats while he went ashore accompanied by ten marines to take Chief Kalaniopuu hostage until the cutter was returned. Kalaniopuu knew the boat no longer existed, but his abductor had grabbed him firmly by the hand, so he had no choice but to go along meekly. The crowds of Hawaiians were shocked to see their chief being treated so sacrilegiously—for even to touch the *alii nui* was a taboo. As one of the chief's wives ran tearfully to him pleading with him not to leave, two chiefs stepped forward to prevent Cook from proceeding, and the elderly chief, trembling with fear, sat down near the water's edge. Meanwhile two chiefs had been approaching the scene in their canoe when the marines guarding the bay entrance opened fire, killing one man, the brother of Palea. The other chief reached shore and shouted news of the murder. Armed warriors, newly dedicated to protect their chiefs under an oath to the war god, Ku, now crowded angrily around Cook. Chief Palea rushed forward, spear held ready, threatening to avenge his brother's death. Cook fired his pistol at him. Quickly another man threw a stone, hitting the captain's forehead, and Cook whirled on the man, killing him with one shot. He then drew his sword and slashed at another chief who grabbed Cook's arms in an effort to restrain him. Cook, struggling, and bleeding from his head wound, groaned aloud as he fell to the ground. Instantly the warriors realized that Cook was not divine, and, infuriated, fell upon him with clubs and stones.

The fifty-year-old Cook had just explored the last unknown archipelago in Oceania—a chain of volcanic mountain tips poking through the blue sheen of the mid Pacific and destined ultimately to become a crossroads of Pacific travel. He had named them the Sandwich Islands, after his patron, the Earl of Sandwich, but the old Hawaiian words for the islands lived on. And for Cook, too, Hawaiians have a word—his time was *pau*—finished, ended—past.

But the time of another man was just beginning. Three years after Cook's death came the death of Paramount Chief Kalaniopuu. His nephew, Kamehameha, dissatisfied with his land inheritance, recruited five other chiefs of Kohala, and together they declared war on the rest of the island. Kamehameha had a vision of an empire. To make his dream a reality he needed guns.

But for seven years no white men appeared. By 1789, American and English fur traders began stopping by to refresh themselves with food, water, and women before continuing on to China with their cargoes of sea otter furs from the cold North Pacific waters. Then traders discovered that Hawaii had something of its own for the China trade—and so the sandalwood rape of the islands began. Where other chiefs accepted rum, cloth, mirrors, even beads in return for harvests of sandalwood, Kamehameha held out for armament; and within fifteen years, he had gathered an arsenal of over six hundred muskets, a dozen or so cannons, and forty other guns. He had also amassed twenty armed sailing ships and he had recruited white adventurers to captain them and to train his army.

The other chiefs now tried to arm themselves against him—but they had realized their danger too late. For eighteen years Kamehameha battled his way through the islands, Hawaii, Maui, Molokai, Lanai, and Oahu, where he drove his opponents up and over the knifelike Pali cliffs. Only Kauai and Niihau still remained free, but finally, in 1810, their *alii nui* also joined the federation. Kamehameha had realized his dream—he alone ruled a united Hawaii.

The year of Kamehameha's death, 1819, saw the beginning of another era in Hawaiian history—the arrival of the first whaling ships. Others followed, and Hawaii soon became known as the isles of plenty for the thirsty, sex-hungry, brawling crews. They brought still other diseases to Hawaii.

One year after the whalers had arrived came the first missionaries, a company of New England Congregationalists. These strict Protestants meant to make converts or break the pagan spirit in trying, and eventually they did both. But first, too much curvaceous golden skin was being sinfully flaunted—quickly the puritan women stitched up enveloping cloth sacks, known today as the muu-muu, a "typical Hawaiian" dress.

King Liholiho refused conversion, fearful of losing his five wives and his liquor supply. And, at first, the dowager queen Kaahumanu, too, scoffed at the new religion—she who had broken the old gods' taboos resisted taking up new ones. Yet she yearned to be able to read and write—and she knew the price. She not only became a convert to Christianity but was soon its staunchest champion. Within ten years, forty thousand Hawaiians were trying to understand missionary-imposed taboos.

King Kamehameha III, on advice from missionaries, repealed the ordinance that had prohibited sale of land to foreigners. Keeping about a million acres for himself, Kamehameha under the land division of the Great Mahele, divided the rest among the government, the alii and the people. Commoners had never owned land before and were soon bilked of it by foreign settlers, missionaries, and other opportunists.

As petroleum had been discovered elsewhere, the price of whale oil fell, and sugarcane took over the Hawaiian economy. During the next twenty years, pressures were put upon the succeeding Kamehameha kings to secure a tariff-free status with the United States for Hawaiian sugar. When the desired treaty was at last signed, it traded duty-free sugar for a naval base at the mouth of the Pearl River.

For centuries Hawaiians had made their houses with sugarcane thatch and chewed the green stalks for their sweetness, but the foreigners now developed the cane into a highly profitable commercial product. Land grabbing alien settlers needed plenty of cheap, willing laborers, and the Hawaiians were unsatisfactory workers; so, too, were Gilbert Islanders and New Hebrideans. The planters had to go all the way to China to get what they wanted. Over forty thousand Chinese were brought into Hawaii during the second half of the nineteenth century. Other sources of "cheap humble labor" were Portuguese, of whom twenty thousand came to the islands; Japanese, numbering nearly two hundred thousand; Filipinos, over a hundred thousand; as well as Koreans, Puerto Ricans, and Spaniards. Sugar was indisputably king.

Under pressure from sugar barons and missionaries, Queen Liliuokalani had been forced to cede the islands to the United States as a territory in 1898. The last Hawaiian monarch died nine years later. The time of Hawaiian alii nui was pau.

There came then, the growing and canning of pineapples. The business began small in 1900, but within less than forty years Hawaii was producing eighty percent of the world's canned pineapple. Then there were coffee and cattle; then there were the army and navy; then there came a bombing and a war. And finally, in 1959, Hawaii became the fiftieth of the United States. As more and more visitors from the mainland arrived, seeking their two-week place in the Hawaiian sun, more and more hotels spawned on the man-made beaches of Oahu, as well as elsewhere throughout the islands.

And what of the Hawaiian? Where in this scheme of progress and wealth are the islanders whose language names the islands, the silent valleys, the snow-tipped mountains, the fiery volcanoes, the hot dog stands, and the world's largest shopping center?

The time of Hawaii for Hawaiians is pau.

# Tonga

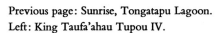

Previous page: Sunrise, Tongatapu Lagoon.
Left: King Taufa'ahau Tupou IV.
Left below: The royal palace at Nuka'alofa.
Below: Royal tortoise.
Opposite: Ha'amonga-a-Maui trilithon.

Below: Young girl, Tongatapu.
Right: High school student, Tongatapu.
Opposite: Rain, Tongatapu.

Above: Drying a large tapa.
Left: Painting designs on tapa.
Opposite below: Tongans in Sunday dress.

Opposite: Roasting pigs for a Sunday feast, Tongatapu.

Above left: Royal flying foxes, Tongatapu.

Above right: Country road, Tongatapu.

Left: Tongan graves, decorated with bottles.

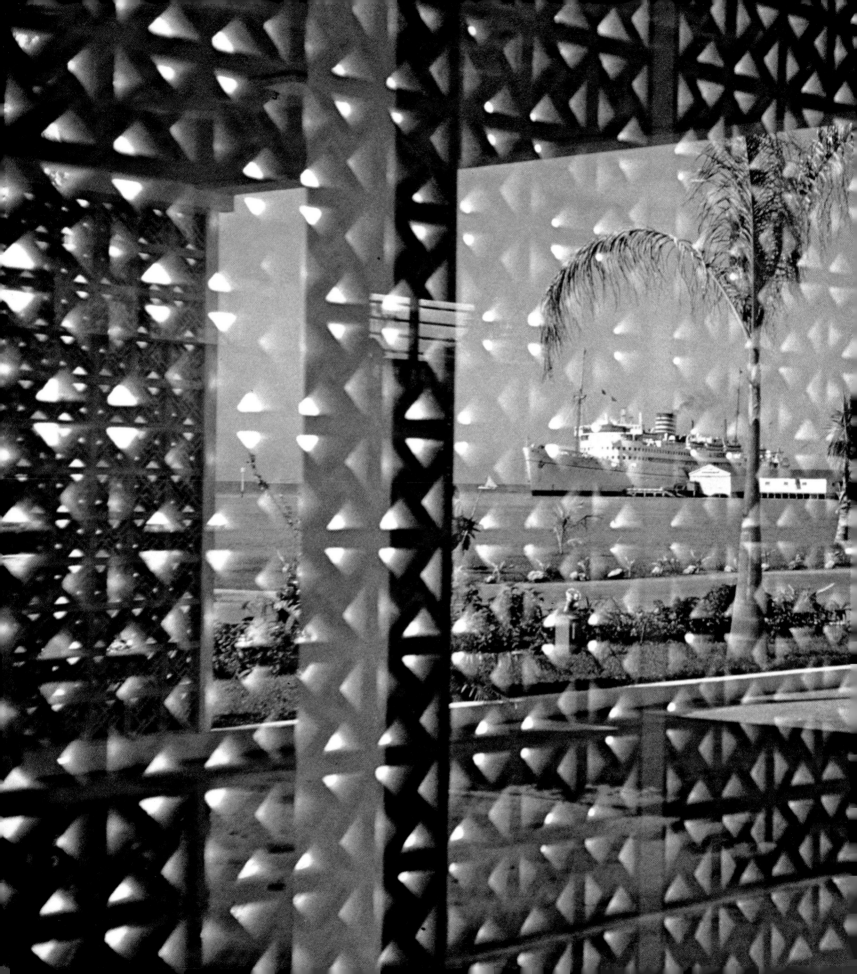

Left: Harbor reflected in International Dateline Hotel window, Tongatapu.
Below: Harbor, Nuku'alofa.

Samoa

Opposite: Pago Pago Harbor, Tutuila.

Right: Steering longboat over reefs, Tau.

Left: Samoan house and chiefs, Tau.
Below: Kava ceremony, Tutuila.

Below: Preparing for a feast, Tutuila.
Opposite left: High Talking Chief, Tau.
Opposite right: Talking Chief Pele and family, Tutuila.

217

Below: Watching a parade, Pago Pago.
Opposite left: Samoan girl dancing the *siva-siva*, Pago Pago.
Opposite right: Samoan entertainers, Pago Pago Intercontinental Hotel.

Left: Launching a new longboat, Pago Pago.

Opposite: Longboat races, Pago Pago Harbor.

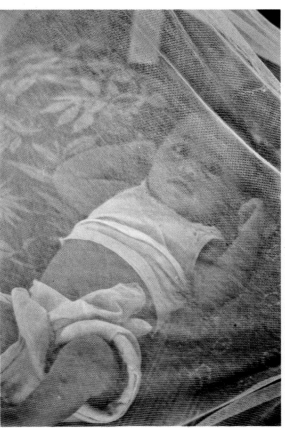

Above: Mother and baby, Swains Island.
Above right: Baby, Swains Island.
Right: Christian church, Tau.
Far right: Horse, Tutuila.

Below: Contemporary Samoa, Pago Pago.
Opposite: Woman and child, Pago Pago.
Overleaf: Throwing a fishnet, Moorea.

# Tahiti

Left: Moorea.
Opposite: Girl wading in a mountain stream.

Opposite: Tahitian women.
Right: Tahitian dancers.

Below: Rowing a longboat over a reef, Tetiaroa Atoll.
Opposite: Fishing, Bora Bora.

Left: Tahitian girl.
Opposite: Aad van der Heyde,
artist, Moorea.
Overleaf: Lagoon, Ra'iatea.

Below: Marae (temple), Moorea.
Right: Sunset, Moorea.

Left: Taro leaf.
Opposite: Cows in lagoon, Tahiti.

Below: Bora Bora, across the lagoon from Tahaa Island.
Opposite: Bora Bora sailing canoe.

# Hawaii

Left: Na Pali coastline, Kauai.
Opposite: Lava cave burial grounds,
Hawaii Island.

Opposite above: Surfers' car, Honolulu.
Opposite below left: Beachboy and son, Waikiki Beach.
Opposite below right: Waikiki Beach beauty.
Below: Surfing, Oahu.

Opposite: Crowd on University of Hawaii campus.
Right: Senior citizens club songfest, Oahu.
Below: Beauty contest winner, Oahu.
Below center: Hawaiian child, Oahu.
Below right: Cowboy, Kauai.

Above: Honolulu at night.
Far left: Artist, Maui.
Left: Fashion show, Honolulu.
Opposite: Porpoise, Kahala Hilton, Oahu.
Overleaf: Sea and sun, Hawaii.